# the total wellbeing diet

Dr. Manny Noakes with Dr. Peter Clifton

PENGUIN CANADA

Published by the Penguin Group

Penguin Group (Canada), 90 Eglinton Avenue East, Suite 700, Toronto, Ontario, Canada M4P 2Y3 (a division of Pearson Canada Inc.)

Penguin Group (USA) Inc., 375 Hudson Street, New York, New York 10014, U.S.A.
Penguin Books Ltd, 80 Strand, London WC2R 0RL, England
Penguin Ireland, 25 St Stephen's Green, Dublin 2, Ireland (a division of Penguin Books Ltd)
Penguin Group (Australia), 250 Camberwell Road, Camberwell, Victoria 3124, Australia (a division of Pearson Australia Group Pty Ltd)
Penguin Books India Pvt Ltd, 11 Community Centre, Panchsheel Park, New Delhi – 110 017, India
Penguin Group (NZ), cnr Airborne and Rosedale Roads, Albany, Auckland 1310, New Zealand (a division of Pearson New Zealand Ltd)
Penguin Books (South Africa) (Pty) Ltd, 24 Sturdee Avenue, Rosebank, Johannesburg 2196, South Africa

Penguin Books Ltd, Registered Offices: 80 Strand, London WC2R 0RL, England

Published in Penguin Canada paperback by Penguin Group (Canada), a division of Pearson Canada Inc., 2006
Simultaneously published in the U.S.A. by New American Library, a division of Penguin Group (USA) Inc.

First published in Australia as *The CSIRO Total Wellbeing Diet* by Penguin Group (Australia), a division of Pearson Australia Group Pty. Ltd., 2005

1 2 3 4 5 6 7 8 9 10

Copyright © CSIRO, 2005

The authors would like to thank the Australian Women's Weekly Test Kitchen for permission to reproduce the following recipes: minestrone with meatballs (page 97); Thai beef salad (page 108); seeded-mustard rack of veal with roasted vegetables (page 159).

The information contained in this book is not intended as a substitute for consulting with your physician or other health care provider. People often have individual requirements or sensitivities such as allergies. This book is not intended to address these factors at an individual level. The publisher, CSIRO, and the authors have taken care in the preparation of this book but do not warrant that the information it contains will be free from errors or omissions, or that it will be suitable for each reader's purposes. The publisher, CSIRO, and the authors are not responsible for specific health or allergy needs or for any adverse medical or other effects, reactions, or consequences resulting from the use of any suggestions or recipes, preparations, procedures, or opinions contained in this book or for any loss or damage allegedly arising from the information or suggestions contained in this book. If you suspect that you have a health, medical, allergy or similar problem or sensitivity, you should consult with a properly qualified medical practitioner.

The recipes contained in this book are to be followed exactly as written. The publisher is not responsible for your specific health or allergy needs that may require medical supervision. The publisher is not responsible for any adverse reactions to the recipes contained in this book.

The publisher does not have any control over and does not assume any responsibility for the author or third-party Web sites or thier content.

Manufactured in the U.S.A.

Library and Archives Canada Cataloguing in Publication

Noakes, Manny, 1953–
    The toal well-being diet / Manny Noakes with Peter Clifton.

Includes index.
ISBN-13: 978-0-14-305664-5
ISBN-10: 0-14-305664-6

    1. Weight loss.    2. Reducing diets.    I. Clifton, Peter (Peter M.)    II. Title.

RM222.2.N597 2006            613.2'5            C2006-900582-6

American Library of Congress Cataloging in Publication data available

Visit the Penguin Group (Canada) website at **www.penguin.ca**

Special and corporate bulk purchase rates available; please see **www.penguin.ca/corporatesales** or call 1-800-399-6858, ext. 477 or 474

# preface

This book from the Commonwealth Scientific and Industrial Research Organization (CSIRO) is about a proven weight-loss program that offers hope to the weight-loss weary with an eating plan that has many benefits. Based on controlled scientific trials that we carried out over several years, the Total Wellbeing Diet is a nutritionally balanced, protein-plus, low-fat eating plan that will change the way you think about losing weight forever. Not only can you lose weight (as much as 2 pounds a week), but you can burn off some of that excess tummy fat, reducing your waistline by inches.

Obesity rates have increased significantly in the U.S. in the past twenty years. It's a fact that today more than 64 percent of American adults 20 years of age and older are overweight or obese. For young people, that statistics are even more dramatic: obesity rates have tripled over the past 20 years and 16 percent of children and teens ages 6–19 are obese. These individuals are vulnerable to a range of chronic illnesses, including heart disease, high blood pressure, stroke, type 2 diabetes and some cancers.

At the same time, it's conservatively estimated that around one-third of American adults are actively trying to lose weight—but are confused about the best way to diet. This is why diet books seem to be bestsellers—most people desperately try them all.

At the CSIRO Clinical Research Unit in Adelaide we were well aware that many people were baffled about what they should or shouldn't eat to lose weight. Should they cut out carbs? Opt for low-fat? Or simply eat soup for a week? We spend a lot of time with our volunteers during our various nutrition and health trials, and the question they constantly ask us is which diet we recommend. They are confused by the contradictory fad diets promoted in the popular media—seemingly a new one every week! What is the best way to lose weight and keep it off, they asked. A low-fat/high-carbohydrate diet? A "revolutionary" high-protein approach? Is carbohydrate rather than fat the culprit in obesity? Is it my blood type? Or is a grapefruit diet really the answer?

Over the years, our Adelaide nutrition laboratories have gained an international reputation in a number of areas. The aim of our research has always been to provide people with practical ways to improve and maintain their good health. We decided it was high time we took a look at how you can maintain optimum health and weight and reduce the risk of diseases like type 2 diabetes and heart disease. The Total Wellbeing Diet has been developed specifically in response to the findings from the research programs that we carried out over a period of years. We asked ourselves which dietary approaches will give you the best results, not only in terms of the amount of weight and fat you lose, but also in terms of your overall health and well-being. What we found was that the way you diet can have a significant impact on how (and where) you lose weight, and on your overall health.

Our findings led us to develop a protein-plus, low-fat eating plan, which we now call the Total Wellbeing Diet. This diet is nutritionally balanced and contains a moderate amount of carbohydrates. It's a low-calorie plan you can follow safely and then readily adapt by adding more foods as a way of eating for life. Unlike some other diets, it does not cut out any food groups.

CSIRO is Australia's national science agency and one of the world's largest and most diverse scientific research organizations. Our research into human health includes such areas as disease prevention, diagnosis and innovative treatment.

This book and the research for the Total Wellbeing Diet occurred thanks to the efforts of many people. First and foremost the following dietitians and nutrition scientists at CSIRO Health Sciences and Nutrition:

- Dr. Katrine Baghurst BSc, PhD
- Jane Bowen BSc (Hons), BND
- Dr. Grant Brinkworth B App Sc (Hons) PhD
- Dr. Michael Fenech PhD (genetic toxicology)
- Dr. Paul Foster BSc, Grad Dip Nut & Diet, Grad Dip Adult & Further Education, PhD
- Jennifer Keogh MSc, Dip Nut Diet
- Dr. David Topping BSc, PhD.

We must also thank the Communication crew at CSIRO— Warrick Glynn, Jan Stokes, and the wonderful team at CSIRO Enquiries who have managed and continue to manage the constant queries about the Total Wellbeing Diet they receive from health professionals and the general public.

The *Australian Women's Weekly* has played a major role in helping us tell the world about our research and the Total Wellbeing Diet. The feedback from the thousands of readers of their August 2003 issue, telling us their stories and how the diet has helped them, has been absolutely inspiring.

Similarly, our professional colleagues Andrea Mortensen and Veronique Droulez from Meat & Livestock Australia have been vital players in helping make the Total Wellbeing Diet happen.

We very gratefully acknowledge all those who have contributed to the funding of our research into higher protein diets for weight management:

- CSIRO Health Sciences and Nutrition
- Dairy Australia
- Goodman Fielder
- Meat & Livestock Australia
- The National Heart Foundation
- The National Centre of Excellence for Functional Foods.

Many thanks to the volunteers who participated in our diet studies. We are indebted to you for your time and goodwill.

We would like to sincerely thank the talented and tireless efforts of Julie Gibbs and her team at Penguin Books, Nicola Young, Susan McLeish and Nikki Townsend, who helped transform our rather factual manuscript into something which we believe brilliantly communicates the essence of the Total Wellbeing Diet.

**Dr. Manny Noakes BSc, Dip Nut Diet, PhD and**
**Dr. Peter Clifton MB BS, B Med Sci, FRACP, MRCP, PhD**

# introduction

As the obesity epidemic loomed, we at the CSIRO realized that scientific research into dietary patterns and weight control was urgently needed. Since 1995, we have conducted a number of controlled trials to find out which dietary approaches will give the best results, not only in terms of the amount of weight and fat you will lose, but also in terms of your overall health and well-being. In our early studies we looked at the amount of dietary fat and what kind of fats dieters should eat for weight loss, at the psychological impacts of dieting, and at how much protein would help dieters control their appetite and prevent muscle loss.

The good news is that losing even a small amount of weight with the right diet can have substantial benefits for total physical well-being—lowering blood pressure, blood glucose levels, LDL cholesterol levels (see page 15) and insulin levels (see page 20). No one drug could have that kind of impact!

## what we found out about fat

We quickly discovered that eating less fat was not the only approach to weight control. Our very low-fat and higher fat diets resulted in equal weight loss, as long as people consumed the same total daily amounts of energy (calories).

We also found, just as previous research had shown, that the type of fat you consume makes a difference to risk factors, such as the concentrations in the blood of LDL and HDL cholesterol (see page 15). In fact, provided our volunteers ate "good," healthy fats, such as those found in nuts, oils and soft margarines, the higher fat weight-loss diets had a better effect on these blood fats than the very low-fat diets (see page 3).

## should you go on a diet or not?

Experts don't agree on the best way to help people lose weight, because there is no such thing as a "best" way—only a best way for you. We tried a number of dietary approaches and a number of ways of helping our volunteers go about them.

One school of thought says it's counterproductive to encourage people to go on a restrictive diet. The concern seems to be that because dieting is normally a short-term activity, many people find it hard to stick to the program in the long term and then regain all the weight lost, plus a bit more. The usual recommendation is to make gradual rather than radical changes to existing eating patterns.

We have to say that we found absolutely no evidence to support this approach for the majority of people. In fact, we found the opposite. Whenever we tried the "take it slow and easy" approach, the results were disappointing on average. This was also the case when we used brochures on weight control that talked generally about healthy eating. Our volunteers had heard it all before. It wasn't what they needed.

In fact, they knew exactly what they wanted—a structured approach that gave them a day-by-day healthy eating program for weight loss, tailored to their calorie needs. As a result, we came up with a diet that included menus and recipes that gave them *structure*, *simplicity* and some (but not too much!) *flexibility*. We also encouraged regular exercise in the form of a brisk walk three times a week. Our volunteers told us that we had "hit the spot" with this approach. And the results bore this out. The people on the trial of the structured approach lost, on average, 1 to 2 pounds per week (sometimes more), while those on the "slow and easy approach" programs only lost less than 1/2 pound per week. Volunteers on the structured diet also felt in control of their eating patterns—and as a result they lost more weight.

## which type of healthy eating pattern is easier to follow?

Since our earlier studies had shown that higher protein meals help control appetite and prevent muscle loss during a dieting regimen, we looked at the overall long-term effects of high-protein diets on weight loss, body fat, muscle distribution,

metabolism, appetite control, kidney and liver function, and bone health. Our positive results with this approach, coupled with the real satisfaction of our volunteers, spurred us on to develop our low-calorie, protein-plus, low-fat eating plan—the Total Wellbeing Diet.

## developing the Total Wellbeing Diet

As we have explained, our initial research had shown that low-calorie weight-loss diets higher in protein were at least as good if not better than high-carbohydrate diets when it came to fat loss and muscle preservation in people with type 2 diabetes (see page 20) or high insulin levels. In our subsequent controlled study with women, we assessed the effectiveness of two different dietary programs: one was a higher protein/low-fat plan and the other a higher carbohydrate/low-fat diet (see opposite: the CSIRO study diets). More than 100 overweight or obese women, half with signs of metabolic syndrome, took part in the trial over a 12-week period, and we followed them up for one year after that.

# the CSIRO study diets

The initial dietary trials at CSIRO assessed the effectiveness of two diets, as follows. Approximately 100 women followed one of the two diets (i.e., 50 women per diet) over a period of 12 weeks. Both diets had a daily calorie count of 1350.

For more information on the results obtained from these studies, see Appendix 4 (page 198).

## 1  Higher protein, low-fat meal plan

This diet contained 34 percent protein (by calorie), 20 percent fat and 46 percent carbohydrate.

**FOOD ALLOWED ON STUDY DIET 1**

| food type | quantity |
| --- | --- |
| high-fiber cereal | 1½ oz/day |
| low-fat milk | 8 oz/day |
| whole grain bread | 2 slices/day |
| fruit | 2 pieces/day |
| lean beef/lamb for dinner | 7 oz/day |
| lean chicken/fish/other meat for lunch | 3.5 oz/day |
| vegetables | 2½ cups/day |
| low-fat yogurt | 8 oz/day |
| canola oil | 3 teaspoons/day |
| wine | 2 glasses/week—optional |

## 2  Higher carbohydrate, low-fat meal plan

This diet contained 17 percent protein, 20 percent fat and 63 percent carbohydrate.

**FOOD ALLOWED ON STUDY DIET 2**

| food type | quantity |
| --- | --- |
| high-fiber cereal | 1½ oz/day |
| low-fat milk | 8 oz/day |
| whole grain bread | 3 slices/day |
| fruit | 3 pieces/day |
| pasta/rice | 3.5 oz cooked/day |
| lean chicken/fish/pork | 3 oz/day |
| vegetables | 2½ cups/day |
| cookies | 3 small cookies/day |
| canola oil | 3 teaspoons/day |
| wine | 2 glasses/week—optional |

We compared the effectiveness of the two diets in relation to how much weight and actual body fat the women lost, and from *where* precisely the fat was lost. This is critical, because excess fat lost from around the tummy area significantly lowers the risk of metabolic syndrome.

The women with signs of metabolic syndrome, or insulin resistance syndrome (see page 4), who were on the higher protein/low-fat diet lost 18 pounds, while those on the higher carbohydrate/low-fat diet lost 13 pounds. More important, the women on the higher protein diet lost twice as much excess fat *around the middle* as those on the higher carbohydrate diet. The women who did not have signs of metabolic syndrome lost a similar amount of weight using either dietary approach. This suggests that the way our metabolism works can make a difference to which diet will be the most effective way for us to lose weight.

We also looked at the impact of the diets on the women's overall health and well-being, including a reduction in the risk of heart disease and diabetes. (See Appendix 4, page 198, for a summary of our results.) For both groups of women, losing weight on either diet helped to reduce their risk of heart disease and diabetes by lowering their triglyceride levels (one of the markers for metabolic syndrome) and reducing their insulin and glucose levels. The higher protein/low-fat diet also helped to control hunger pangs. This is because protein-rich foods like lean red meat, chicken and fish have a high satiety value (they keep you feeling fuller for longer). Women on the higher protein diet found it easier to stick to the diet long term too—the number of drop-outs on the higher carbohydrate/low-fat diet was three times greater than on the higher protein/low-fat diet.

## understanding metabolic syndrome

At least one in four Americans has metabolic syndrome (or insulin resistance syndrome), many without even knowing it. Metabolic syndrome is generally characterized by excess fat around the tummy, high blood pressure, high insulin levels, high blood glucose levels, high blood triglyceride levels and low blood levels of HDL or "good cholesterol." People with metabolic syndrome are at greater risk of developing heart disease and type 2 diabetes. However, if you are predisposed to metabolic syndrome, you can prevent its development by losing weight (as little as 7–9 pounds will make a difference), eating healthily and exercising.

For a clinical diagnosis of metabolic syndrome, you are likely to have three or more of the following symptoms.

**SYMPTOMS OF METABOLIC SYNDROME**

| symptom | women | men |
|---|---|---|
| waist circumference | greater than 35 inches | greater than 40 inches |
| triglycerides | greater than 150 mg/dL | greater than 150 mg/dL |
| blood pressure | greater than 130/85 | greater than 130/85 |
| HDL cholesterol | less than 50 mg/dL | less than 40 mg/dL |
| fasting glucose | greater than 110 mg/dL | greater than 110 mg/dL |

Other characteristics of metabolic syndrome are sometimes used in diagnosis, for example a high blood insulin level.

## the next steps

Once we had established that the Total Wellbeing Diet had the edge in weight loss over a high-carbohydrate/low-fat diet, and was also a very healthy eating pattern for anyone who wanted to make a positive lifestyle change, it was time to share our findings. In 2003, in partnership with the *Australian Women's Weekly* and Meat & Livestock Australia, we published the Total Wellbeing Diet, along with a two-week menu plan, recipes and recipe tips in the August 2003 issue of the *Weekly*. The response was huge. We were inundated with inquiries and questions from readers who wanted to know more about the Diet and specifically wanted more recipes and menu plans. Many newspapers published our menu plans and guidelines, and each time the response was phenomenal. Our Communication team at CSIRO was dealing with many inquiries for more information and was bending under the strain. That's why we've written this book.

We have set out the book in four parts. In Part 1: Understanding the Total Wellbeing Diet, we show you how you can achieve your weight goals and how the diet can form the basis of lifelong health. We explain what you'll be eating and why, and show you, step by step, how easy the diet plan is to follow. This is not a "one diet fits all" program. There are four levels based on an individual's daily calorie needs. We show you how to calculate your daily calorie intake for your weight-loss goals. We also look at exercise—the crucial other side of the weight-loss equation. There are some pretty compelling arguments in favor of regular exercise. Not only does it increase your metabolism and help you burn fat, but it helps you sustain weight loss, sleep better and fight off depression.

And that's just for starters. In Part 2: Menu plans for the Total Wellbeing Diet, we give you 12 weeks of menus to get you started. In Part 3: Recipes for the Total Wellbeing Diet, we present 100 delicious protein-plus, low-fat recipes you'll want to prepare and eat time and again.

Losing excess pounds is one thing, but we all know that the real challenge is maintaining your new low weight. You've worked so hard to achieve your goal, it would be a shame to let it slide. Once you've reached your goal, you can begin to add foods so that you maintain your weight loss. This is what we cover in Part 4: Maintaining your new low weight, along with some smart tactics to help you keep your eye on the prize.

## Testimonials from people who are using the Total Wellbeing Diet

"I find the diet very easy to follow as it has all the foods that I love. I was initially concerned about the amounts of meat required, as I was never a big meat eater. But I have grown used to buying and eating more meat. The big thing in the program is that it discourages between-meal snacks and I find that this is not a burden. I actually eat far more on this program than I was prior to going on it. I would have considered myself a healthy eater, with lots of fruit and vegetables in the diet, but the increase in protein does appear to have made the difference."
—*Anne*

"I thought I should write to tell you of a 'quiet revolution' that is happening in our country town. We have actively promoted your diet. Our local butcher shop owners—who are on the diet—have of their own volition tailored many of their products to suit the diet. At our surgery we cannot keep up with the requests for photocopies of the diet. The results are really quite astounding. Weight losses in the order of 35–45 pounds over a period of 6–12 months are now becoming common. I have encouraged the type 2 diabetics to use the diet as well, and there are obvious falls in their HbA1c levels. Patients love the diet and the way it is set out—that is a very strong point. The other major comments are: 'I am never hungry' and 'I continue to feel better even after being on the diet for weeks.'"
—*Dr. John*

"After Christmas, my husband and I came back from holidays and jumped on the scales, and much to our horror, weighed much more than when we left. At 35 years of age, we both took a good look at our weight and decided we needed to do something serious. I am the mother of two children (2 and 4 years of age). Even though I only put on 15 pounds during each of my pregnancies (I worked on my feet 10 hours a day until the morning both children were born), I found that I couldn't get down to my ideal weight of 110 pounds (I am only 4'11" tall). I weighed 130 pounds. My husband is 5'9" tall and weighed 225 pounds after Christmas. He never looked fat, but was always referred to as 'stocky' and 'heavily framed.' He has been playing Australian Rules football for as long as I have known him, and even with all his training could not lose any weight. Even our doctor was surprised when we would go in for a yearly checkup, as he could never believe the weight on the scales. Our doctor never suggested that my husband needed to lose weight. Anyway, while on holidays, we saw your 'diet' in the *Herald Sun* and decided that was what we would do. To cut a long story short, we did the post-Christmas diet for the first four weeks, and to our surprise, we had lost 24 pounds between us. We no longer craved the pastas or the potatoes for dinner. We have saved lots of money by making our lunch every day and eating what is on the menu. Today, after 3 months on the 'healthy eating plan' (this is what I tell my family and friends), I currently weigh 111 pounds and my husband weighs 196 pounds. We look fantastic, feel great and have received so many compliments. We feel 20 years old again. So I am writing this letter to say thank you, and we tell all our friends about it, as we are living evidence that it does work. By the way, we are still living by the diet, but are flexible as well when we go out to dinner or eat at friends' houses."
—*Brenda and Russell*

"My doctor diagnosed me with elevated blood pressure, cholesterol and blood glucose due to being overweight. I have been following this eating plan now for 11 weeks, and have lost 18 pounds and 12 inches around my waist. My other problems are now back to normal and there is no need for medication. Thank you."
—*Stacy*

"I wish to extend my gratitude to the people at the CSIRO who came up with this diet. For the last few years I have had a lot of difficulty in controlling my weight and I was at the point of being totally disheartened. My husband saw details of the diet in the *Herald Sun* newspaper and we both thought that we would give it a try for at least a week to see what effect it would have. We are now into our fifth week, and both of us have lost 19 pounds each! We still have a fair distance to go before we get to our ideal weights, but I felt that I needed to say a very big thank you to CSIRO for helping us to make a change."
—*Belinda*

# part one

## understanding the Total Wellbeing Diet

# the Total Wellbeing Diet

## why lose weight?

It's important to be concerned about how much you weigh. The health implications of being overweight and inactive are many: heart disease, high blood pressure, arthritis, osteoporosis, infertility, insulin resistance and type 2 diabetes (a condition that is rapidly increasing as America gets fatter; see page 20) can all be traced to carrying excess pounds. And apart from the wider health considerations, being within your healthy weight range helps you look and feel better all round. It's also not rocket science that exercise is good for your health.

You don't need us to tell you that being overweight doesn't feel great. But you don't need to be skinny to be healthy—just a little thinner than you are now will make a big difference. Unrealistic expectations are just demoralizing. Always set your sights on losing the first few pounds and look at it as a great success if you keep them off for a year or more. If you do better than that, brilliant! But don't give yourself a hard time if you don't make it immediately. Be forgiving.

Depending on your weight, losing just a few pounds can make a huge difference to the way your body functions. Even a weight loss as small as 7–9 pounds, if it is maintained in the long term, can help prevent type 2 diabetes. Well before the scales have started to register a downward movement, your body has responded to eating less. Within 24 hours of cutting down, there are already significant improvements in your blood pressure, blood glucose levels, blood insulin levels, and cholesterol levels.

Eating less can also slow down aging, heart disease and many other chronic diseases. This is because eating too much can cause damage to our DNA. The ability of our bodies to repair this damage is even more compromised if we don't eat enough protective foods. No one yet understands quite how this happens, but we know enough to say that putting on weight is harming us in more ways than we originally thought! Isn't slowing down the aging process a great incentive to be a little more choosy about how much and what we eat?

Losing weight, whether you need to lose a few pounds or a lot, doesn't have to be a battle. It should be about eating well and incorporating more exercise into your life. The Total Wellbeing Diet is a nutritionally balanced eating plan that has been medically and scientifically tested. Not only that, we have designed it so that you can tailor your daily calorie intake to achieve your personal weight-loss goals. As we said before, it's not a "one diet fits all" program.

## what sets the Total Wellbeing Diet apart?

First of all, it's important to note that the Total Wellbeing Diet is a protein-plus, low-fat diet and bears virtually no resemblance to other popular high-protein diets you may have heard about.

The Total Wellbeing Diet is not a very low-carb diet. In fact it contains moderate lower amounts of slow-release carbohydrates (the ones with a low GI; see page 53) that are essential for energy and for maintaining your blood glucose levels. It is nutritionally balanced and can be maintained effectively in the long term.

**AMOUNT OF CARBOHYDRATE CONSUMED IN DIFFERENT DIETS**

| type of diet | g of carbohydrate consumed per day | % of calories in diet coming from carbohydrate |
| --- | --- | --- |
| low-fat | greater than 200 | greater than 55 |
| very low-carbohydrate (e.g., Atkins) | less than 100 | less than 20 |
| moderate to low carbohydrate (e.g., Total Wellbeing Diet) | 100–200 | 20–40 |
| average nondiet intake | 245 | 45 |

What sets the Total Wellbeing Diet apart is that it has been tested on hundreds of people since 1997 and is more than just a weight-loss strategy; it is a protein-plus, low-fat eating plan that can help you lose weight and keep it off.

We based our diet on clinically tested research information that clearly indicated protein foods are more satisfying than fats or carbohydrate, are helpful in maintaining muscle, and are good for heart health. Although we built the menus for your daily calorie needs around protein foods, we also included plenty of grains, fruits and vegetables, and "good" fats, to pack as much healthy eating as possible into your daily calorie allowance. Although protein foods are a rich source of nutrients, the additional foods were vital in adding fiber, vitamin C and B vitamins, along with a host of free-radical-fighting antioxidants.

So although you may be eating less when you are on the Total Wellbeing Diet than you usually do, you shouldn't feel too many hunger pangs, and your body will reap the health benefits. Take a look opposite at the snapshot of how just one day on our protein-plus, low-fat eating plan looks. No need for a vitamin pill here. Each food has been carefully chosen to provide you with maximum nutrition.

## Just one day

Here's a snapshot of how Day 1 on the Total Wellbeing Diet might look.

## Breakfast

1½ oz high-fiber breakfast cereal (e.g., Fiber One) with 8 oz low-fat milk and 1 sliced banana

Breakfast = 1 unit cereal (see page 22), 1 unit dairy, 1 unit fruit

## Lunch

Salmon and salad sandwich (2 slices whole grain bread with 2 tsp margarine, 3.5 oz salmon and ½ cup salad leaves)

Lunch = 2 units bread, 2 units fats, 1 unit protein, ½ unit veggies

## Dinner

7 oz beef: Char-grilled Beef Filet with Mushrooms* (see page 157)

½ cup steamed beans drizzled with ½ tsp olive oil

¾ cup fresh fruit with 7 oz low-fat custard

Dinner = 2 units protein, 2 units veggies, 1 unit fats, 1 unit fruit, 1 unit dairy

## Snack options

tea or coffee with low-fat milk

1 cup low-calorie soup

| | |
|---|---|
| 1 unit cereal, 2 units bread | contains fiber, slow-release carbohydrate, B vitamins, magnesium |
| 2 units dairy | contains calcium, protein, vitamin B12, zinc |
| 2½ units veggies, 2 units fruit | contains folate, vitamins A, B6 and C, fiber, magnesium, antioxidants |
| 3 units protein | red meat contains protein, well-absorbed iron, zinc, vitamin B12; fish contains protein, omega-3 fatty acids |
| 3 units fats | oils and margarines contain vitamin E; margarine contains vitamins A and D |

*For recipes, see pages 89–185. All recipes have been written for this diet and adhere to the principles of the diet. See individual recipes for the amount of each allowed food type they contain. For example, Char-grilled Beef Filet with Mushrooms contains 2 units protein, 1½ units vegetables and ½ unit fats.

# discover the long-term health benefits of the Total Wellbeing Diet

What we eat has a powerful impact on the way our body functions—it affects everything from our weight and our heart and bone health to our skin, hair and even our mood.

Nutrition scientists and researchers are discovering more about "food as medicine" every day, helping to challenge long-held, and sometimes just plain wrong beliefs. For instance, we now know that a totally fat-free diet is not smart. Our bodies need a certain amount of "good" or unsaturated fat (from nuts, seeds, olives and avocados, for example) to function properly and thrive.

We now know more about the real health benefits of a higher protein diet.

### • Protein-rich foods provide us with many important nutrients

Lean red meat, poultry, fish, dairy foods and eggs are excellent sources of a wide range of nutrients essential for long-term health and vitality. Lean red meat (beef, lamb and veal) is the richest source of well-absorbed iron, which helps move oxygen around our bodies and is essential for normal brain development and function. Red meats are also a useful source of omega-3 fats and are rich in zinc, which helps boost our immune system. Because our bodies are better able to absorb zinc and iron from meat rather than plant foods, we included red meat in our diet 4 times a week. Fish and seafood are important sources of omega-3 fats, which help protect the heart.

Dairy foods such as low-fat milk, yogurt and cheese are also rich in protein, riboflavin (vitamin B2) and calcium (in fact, 2–3 units ensure you will achieve your daily calcium requirements, vital for strong bones). Eggs contain protein, vitamins A, D and E and B-group vitamins, as well as the minerals iron, phosphorus and zinc. They're relatively low in saturated fat, and are also an important source of antioxidants.

Lean red meat, poultry, fish, dairy and eggs are all excellent sources of vitamin B12, a micronutrient that plays a key role in protecting our DNA and nervous system.

### • Protein-rich foods help you feel satisfied for longer

Protein-rich foods such as lean red meat, poultry and fish will keep the hunger pangs at bay for much longer. Their high satiety value means that you feel fuller longer. This makes it easier to stick to a high-protein diet than to one that leaves you itching to break into the cookie jar.

### • Protein-rich foods help control your blood fats

This diet can result in a significant reduction in triglycerides and LDL (bad) cholesterol in the blood (see page 15). So if you're worried that adding more protein to your meals will increase your cholesterol levels, don't be. Just remember to choose lean cuts of red meat, remove skin from chicken, and opt for reduced-fat dairy products.

## Blood cholesterol and your health

A high blood level of cholesterol is a major risk factor for coronary heart disease, heart attack and stroke. It causes atherosclerosis, a slow, complex disease that starts in childhood and often progresses with age—in some people rapidly. It is thought to begin with damage to the innermost layer of the artery, three proven causes of which are:

- elevated levels of blood cholesterol and triglycerides
- high blood pressure, and
- tobacco smoke.

Tobacco smoke greatly worsens atherosclerosis and speeds its growth.

### what is LDL cholesterol?

LDL (low-density lipoprotein) cholesterol is the major cholesterol carrier in the blood. It carries 60–80 percent of the body's cholesterol. Some of this is used by tissues to build cells and some is returned to the liver. If too much LDL cholesterol circulates in the blood, it can slowly build up on the walls of the arteries that feed the heart and brain.

Together with other substances, LDL cholesterol can form "plaque" and contribute to atherosclerosis. That's why LDL cholesterol is often called "bad" cholesterol. Lower levels of LDL cholesterol in the blood reflect a lower risk of heart disease.

### what is HDL cholesterol?

One-third to one-quarter of blood cholesterol is carried by HDL (high-density lipoprotein) cholesterol. It is produced primarily in the liver and intestines, and released into the bloodstream. HDL cholesterol removes excess cholesterol from atherosclerotic plaques and thus slows their growth. HDL cholesterol is "good" cholesterol because in high levels it seems to protect against heart attack; people with low HDL cholesterol levels have a higher risk of heart attack and perhaps stroke.

### HDL and triglyceride levels

As a rule, women have higher HDL cholesterol levels than men. The female sex hormone, estrogen, tends to raise HDL cholesterol, which may help explain why premenopausal women are usually protected from heart disease. Estrogen production is highest during the childbearing years.

As people get older, fatter or both, their triglyceride (another fat in the blood) and cholesterol levels rise. Many people with heart disease or diabetes have high triglyceride levels. A high triglyceride level combined with low HDL cholesterol or high LDL cholesterol seems to speed up atherosclerosis.

The following controllable risk factors can be reduced:
- high blood cholesterol
- cigarette smoking and exposure to tobacco smoke
- high blood pressure
- type 2 diabetes
- obesity, and
- physical inactivity.

# the Total Wellbeing Diet: your questions answered

### • Is the Total Wellbeing Diet easy to follow?

You should find the diet easy to follow and maintain. The suggested meals won't be very different from what you're used to, and we have included lots of tasty recipes to try (see pages 89–185). To make it even simpler, we provide you not only with the basic principles of the eating plan, but also with menu plans (see page 63) and shopping lists (see page 203) to take the hard work out of choosing what to eat. Maintaining the daily checklist on page 195 will also help you stay on track.

### • Will I get hungry?

On our protein-plus diet you are less likely to get hungry. It has been scientifically proven that high-protein foods are more satisfying than high-fat or high-carbohydrate foods. Of course, we don't always eat only because we are hungry—but when we are actively trying to lose weight, hunger can be a problem. Not only does our eating plan include a sustaining level of protein—from lean red meat, chicken, fish, dairy foods and eggs—it also contains some good slow-release low-GI carbohydrate foods (see page 53), which can also curb hunger.

### • Is the diet flexible enough for me to eat out?

Eating out is okay as long as you follow our guidelines for choosing from the menu. It is often easier to eat higher protein meals when eating out, since most main meals tend to be protein-based dishes. See page 24 for some hints and guidelines for eating out.

### • Will it be bad for my health?

Losing even a few pounds can have a positive effect on your health. Our protein-plus diet has been tested for its effects on kidney, liver and bone health, and we have seen no adverse effects. If you have any preexisting medical condition, such as diabetes, or are taking medication, check with your doctor first, to ensure the eating plan is right for you.

### • Will it help me keep the weight off?

Because this diet is easy to follow and can help you control your hunger, it is more sustainable in the longer term. Once you have reached a weight you feel comfortable with, you can switch to the maintenance plan (see page 189), which allows greater flexibility. But your weight will only stay low if you continue to exercise and take care with your food choices. Keep at it, and don't panic if you fall "off the wagon" occasionally.

### • Will I be able to feed my whole family with the suggested meals?

Yes, you can. The recipes fit easily into family meal plans. However, members of the family who do not need to lose weight may need to include extra carbohydrate foods with their meals, such as bread, pasta, rice or potatoes.

### • Is the diet suitable for children?

The diet is adequate for overweight children from a nutritional perspective as long as it contains 3 units of dairy foods. However, the level of calories will need to be adjusted for the age, size and activity of the child, which is best done by a qualified dietitian. Because children are growing, excessive calorie restriction can retard growth, so some care needs to be taken to ensure their diet is not overly restrictive. We would recommend smaller weight losses per week than for adults, unless the child is very overweight. Sometimes even keeping a child's weight stable as they grow will result in fat loss. If the whole family is eating meals based on the Total Wellbeing Diet, this will provide good nutrition for everyone. Extra snacks (mostly fruit and low-fat dairy snacks) may be necessary for some overweight children. We recommend you consult with your doctor and seek a referral to a dietitian, who will keep an eye on your child's weight and growth.

• **Will I get bored with the meals?**
We have designed the Diet to include a wide variety of foods, with plenty of menu plans and food ideas. Of course there are some indulgence foods that we don't feature—and these have been left out on purpose. However, if you need a treat, choose a mini version of what takes your fancy, savor it slowly and enjoy!

• **Do I need to count calories every day?**
You don't need to count a thing. We have done all the counting for you. However, you do need to keep track of the foods you eat each day. Copy the checklist on page 195 and keep it handy.

• **Do I need to exercise?**
There's no doubt about it—exercise is essential for good health whether or not you are overweight. As a nation we simply have to get active. We appreciate that some people may find exercising difficult, especially if they are overweight. If this is you, be assured that as you lose weight, it will become easier to exercise. However, it is important that you take a walk as briskly as possible for 30 minutes at least 3 times a week. To get started, check out Chapter 2: Energy Balance & Exercise.

## do you need to lose weight?

Most people know if they need to lose weight, but sometimes a reference point can help you be realistic about how much you really need to lose. By using a calculation known as the Body Mass Index (BMI) and measuring your waist circumference, you can roughly assess whether you need to lose weight.

### Body Mass Index (BMI)
BMI is a reasonable but not perfect indicator of body fat. It can be calculated using pounds and inches or kilograms and meters using the following equations:

BMI = weight in kilograms/(height in meters)$^2$
BMI = [weight in pounds/(height in inches)$^2$] x 703

*Example*

Yvonne weighs 100 kg and is 1.63 m (163 cm) tall. Her BMI would therefore be:

100 divided by 1.63 squared: $100/(1.63)^2 = 37.6$

*Example*

Chuck weighs 220 lb and is 6 foot 3 inches tall. His height in inches would be (6 x 12) + 3 = 75. His BMI would therefore be:

220 divided by 75 squared, all multiplied by 703:
$[220/75^2]$ x 703 = 27.5

Once you have calculated your BMI, you can use the following table to determine whether you are overweight or obese.

**WHAT YOUR BMI TELLS YOU**

| BMI | body condition |
|---|---|
| less than 18.5 | underweight |
| 18.5–24.9 | normal |
| 25.0–29.9 | overweight |
| greater than 29.9 | obese |

**Note:** The BMI can be used for both men and women but has the following limitations.

- It can overestimate body fat in athletes and people with a muscular build.
- It can underestimate body fat in older people and others who have lost muscle mass.
- The cut-offs are not applicable to all ethnic groups. For example, in people of Asian ancestry, excess fat may be present at lower BMI values.

## Waist circumference

Waist circumference is another valuable way of assessing whether you need to lose weight. It is a useful gauge of how risky your excess body fat may be. If you are overweight according to your BMI calculation and you also have a waist circumference greater than 40 inches for men or 35 inches for women, it is even more important for you to lose some weight. Increased waist circumference can be a marker for increased risk of type 2 diabetes, hypertension and heart disease, even in people of normal weight.

**BMI, WAIST CIRCUMFERENCE AND ASSOCIATED DISEASE RISKS\***

| body condition | BMI (lbs ÷ in²) × 703 | waist circumference | |
|---|---|---|---|
| | | less than 40 inches (men)/35 inches (women) | greater than 40 inches (men)/35 inches (women) |
| underweight | less than 18.5 | – | – |
| normal | 18.5–24.9 | – | – |
| overweight | 25.0–29.9 | increased | high |
| obese | 30.0–34.9 | high | very high |
| | 35.0–39.9 | very high | very high |
| extremely obese | greater than 39.9 | extremely high | extremely high |

\* Disease risk for type 2 diabetes, hypertension and heart disease.

## Healthy weight ranges

If you don't want to do your own calculations, use this approximate ideal weight-for-height table, adapted from the USDA Dietary Guidelines, but remember that it is only approximate! **Yo-yo dieters usually have higher weights, greater psychological distress, more binge-eating and lower levels of physical activity. If this sounds like you, we strongly recommend you seek psychological support as you embark on a lifestyle change.**

**HEALTHY WEIGHT RANGE (FOR MEN AND WOMEN)**

| height | healthy weight range (in lbs) |
|--------|-------------------------------|
| 4'10" | 91–115 |
| 4'11" | 94–119 |
| 5'0" | 97–123 |
| 5'1" | 100–127 |
| 5'2" | 104–131 |
| 5'3" | 107–135 |
| 5'4" | 110–140 |
| 5'5" | 114–144 |
| 5'6" | 118–148 |
| 5'7" | 121–153 |
| 5'8" | 125–158 |
| 5'9" | 126–162 |
| 5'10" | 132–167 |
| 5'11" | 136–172 |
| 6'0" | 140–177 |
| 6'1" | 144–182 |
| 6'2" | 148–186 |
| 6'3" | 152–192 |

Even if you don't get to your ideal weight, if you are overweight, any sustained weight loss is good for your health

## Type 2 diabetes

Type 2 diabetes is a disease in which the body does not produce or properly use insulin. Insulin is a hormone that is needed to convert sugar, starches and other food into energy for daily activities. If you have type 2 diabetes, your blood glucose levels increase, which can harm your large and small blood vessels. The cause of diabetes continues to be a mystery, although genetic factors are involved. Lifestyle factors such as becoming overweight and doing little exercise are also important.

Some diabetes symptoms include:

- increased fatigue
- skin infections and itchiness
- irritability
- blurry vision
- frequent urination
- excessive thirst
- extreme hunger, and
- unusual weight loss.

People most at risk of type 2 diabetes include:

- people over 55 years
- people with a family history of diabetes
- women who have had diabetes during pregnancy
- people (including children) who are overweight
- people with high blood pressure
- people with heart disease, and
- people over 35 of African-American, Latino, Native-American, Chinese, Indian, Maori or Pacific Island heritage.

To test for diabetes, your blood glucose level is measured after you have fasted overnight. You are then given a measured dose of glucose and your blood glucose is measured again after a given period, usually 2 hours. Your blood glucose levels are then compared with the values in the table below.

**GLUCOSE LEVELS FOR DIAGNOSIS OF TYPE 2 DIABETES IN NON-PREGNANT ADULTS**

| condition of glucose metabolism | fasting plasma glucose (mg/dL) | plasma glucose 2 hours after 75 g glucose load (mg/dL) |
|---|---|---|
| normal | less than 110 | less than 140 |
| prediabetes | 110–125 | 140–199 |
| diabetes | greater than 126 | greater than 200 |

According to the American Diabetes Organization National Diabetes Fact Sheet for 2002:

- for every known case of diabetes, there are two undiagnosed cases.
- about 18 million Americans, or 6.3 percent of the total population, have diabetes.
- 1.3 million people age 20 or older are diagnosed with diabetes each year.
- in addition to the 18.2 million Americans diagnosed with diabetes, 41 million Americans have prediabetes.

The early detection and treatment of diabetes is vital, as the complications include heart disease, blindness, kidney disease, poor wound healing, poor circulation (sometimes necessitating limb amputations) and impotence, just to name a few.

Type 2 diabetes can be prevented by managing your weight through regular exercise and a healthy diet.

## following the Total Wellbeing Diet

Here's a rundown of the foods you'll be eating while following our protein-plus, low-fat eating plan. It's a good idea to stick as closely as possible to the day-by-day menu plans (see page 63) for the first 4 weeks, to familiarize yourself with your new way of eating. There's plenty of scope to be more adventurous as you lose weight and move on to the maintenance plan!

It's important to note that the diet incorporates food from each of the food groups, ensuring you don't miss out on any essential nutrients.

**TOTAL WELLBEING DIET—MACRONUTRIENT BREAKDOWN**

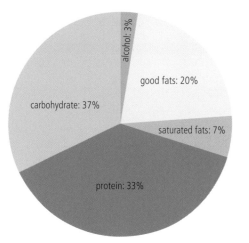

- alcohol: 3%
- good fats: 20%
- carbohydrate: 37%
- saturated fats: 7%
- protein: 33%

We have found that keeping a daily checklist is a great way to stay on track. Copy the checklist on page 195 and keep it handy. You can eat the foods listed on each day's plan at any time during that day, but many people find it easier to stick to a routine.

The Day 1 menu on page 13 is a good guide for putting a day's foods together. The detailed menu plans are also just a guide, but they are a great help if you don't want to have to think too much about what to eat and when.

# the Total Wellbeing Diet

## your daily food allowance

### 1 LEAN PROTEIN FOODS
– 2 units a day for dinner

1 unit is equal to 3.5 oz raw weight of any protein food. Eat 2 units lean red meat (beef, lamb or veal) for dinner 4 times each week. We recommend 2 units fish for dinner twice a week and 2 units fat-trimmed, skinless chicken for dinner one night a week.

### 2 LEAN PROTEIN FOODS
– 1 unit a day for lunch

Eat a 3.5 oz (raw weight) unit of any lean protein source (canned or fresh fish or seafood, chicken, pork, ham, beef, lamb or turkey) each day. You can replace one 3.5 oz lean protein unit with any one of the following:

- 2 eggs
- an extra unit from the dairy group and 1½ oz lean protein

### 3 WHOLE GRAIN BREAD
– 2 units a day

1 unit is equal to one slice. You can replace *one* unit each day with any of the following:

- 2 crispbread, such as Ryvita
- 1 medium potato (about 5 oz)
- ⅓ cup cooked rice or noodles
- ½ cup cooked pasta
- ⅓ cup baked beans, or cooked lentils, kidney beans or other legumes

### 4 HIGH-FIBER CEREAL
– 1 unit a day

1 unit is equal to:

- 1½ oz any high-fiber breakfast cereal (e.g., Raisin Bran, Fiber One)
- 1 biscuit Original Shredded Wheat or Weetabix plus ½ cup All-Bran
- 1 slice whole grain toast

### 5 DAIRY
– 2–3 units a day

1 unit is equal to:

- 8 oz low-fat milk
- 8 oz low-fat or diet yogurt
- 8 oz low-fat custard or dairy dessert
- 1 oz cheddar cheese or other full-fat cheese
- 2 oz reduced-fat cheese (less than 10 percent fat)

If you are lactose-intolerant, use similar quantities of low-fat soy milk products.

### 6 FRUIT
– 2 units a day

You can eat fresh or canned, unsweetened fruit. 1 unit is equal to one piece of fresh fruit, 5 oz of unsweetened canned fruit or 5 oz of unsweetened fruit juice.

## 7 VEGETABLES

– 2½ units a day from free list (at least)

1 unit is equal to 1 cup cooked vegetables. See free list opposite for vegetables you can eat. We recommend ½ unit salad and 2 units cooked vegetables each day.

## 8 FATS AND OILS

– 3 units added oils or fats a day

1 unit is equal to 1 teaspoon any liquid oil such as canola, olive or sunflower oil. 3 units oil is equal to:

* 3 teaspoons soft margarine (note 2 teaspoons light margarine = 1 teaspoon oil)
* 3 teaspoons curry paste in canola oil
* 2 oz avocado
* 1 oz nuts or seeds
* 3 teaspoons peanut butter

## 9 LOW-CALORIE SOUP

– 8 oz a day (optional)

## 10 WINE EXTRAS

—2 glasses (10 oz) a week

A 5 oz glass of wine is equal to:

* 12 oz beer, 1.5 oz liquor
* any snack food that contains about 200 calories, such as 2 oz chocolate. You can have anything that matches that calorie level once a week instead of wine.

## The free list

These foods contain minimal calories, so eat them freely to spice up your meals.

**vegetables** artichokes, asparagus, beansprouts, beets, bok choy, broccoli, Brussels sprouts, cabbage, carrots, cauliflower, celery, chayote, chili peppers, chives, corn, cucumber, fennel, green beans, lettuce, mushrooms, onion, parsnips, peas, peppers, radishes, rhubarb, rutabagas, spinach, squash, Swiss chard, tomatoes, turnip, zucchini

**drinks** clear beef broth, cocoa, coffee, diet soft drinks, herbal tea, tea, unflavored mineral water, water

**condiments** artificial sweeteners, barbecue sauce, chili pepper sauce, curry powder or paste, diet jelly, diet topping, fish sauce, garlic, ginger, herbs, hoisin sauce, horseradish, lemon, mint sauce, mustard, oil-free salad dressing, parsley, pickles, soy sauce, spices, stock cubes, tomato sauce, tomato paste, vinegar, wasabi

**Note:** It is acceptable to use small amounts of cornstarch, tapioca or sugar to thicken or sweeten dishes. 1 level teaspoon cornstarch, tapioca or sugar has 10–15 calories. This is low enough not to worry about if you only use them occasionally. Always use salt sparingly.

**NUTRIENT ANALYSIS OF A TYPICAL DAY ON THE TOTAL WELLBEING DIET BASIC PLAN**

| key foods | amount | calories | protein (g) | fat (g) | saturated fat (g) | carbohydrate (g) | fiber (g) |
|---|---|---|---|---|---|---|---|
| lean dinner protein foods | 7 oz | 258 | 41 | 10 | 4.0 | 0 | 0 |
| lean lunch protein foods | 3.5 oz | 128 | 20.5 | 5 | 2.0 | 0 | 0 |
| whole grain bread | 2.5 oz | 165 | 7 | 3 | 0.4 | 27 | 4.6 |
| high-fiber cereal | 1½ oz | 102 | 3 | 1 | 0.1 | 18 | 10.0 |
| fruit | 10 oz | 120 | 2 | 0 | 0 | 28 | 5.7 |
| low-fat milk | 8 oz | 126 | 10 | 4 | 2.3 | 14 | 0 |
| low-fat yogurt/dairy dessert | 8 oz | 102 | 10 | 0 | 0.2 | 12 | 0 |
| vegetables | 2 cups | 105 | 7 | 1 | 0 | 9 | 9.0 |
| salad | ½ cup | 17 | 1 | 0 | 0 | 2 | 2.1 |
| oil | 3 teaspoons | 133 | 0 | 15 | 1.1 | 0 | 0 |
| low-calorie soup | 8 oz | 29 | 1 | 1 | 0.4 | 4 | 0.5 |
| wine | 1.5 oz | 34 | 0 | 0 | 0 | 0 | 0 |
| **TOTAL** | — | **1319** | **102.5** | **40** | **10.5** | **114** | **31.9** |

## tips for eating out

Just because you're watching your weight doesn't mean you need to hide yourself away from the world. In fact, dining out is a great way to test what you've learned and to prove to yourself that it is possible to eat healthily and enjoy life at the same time. Try to limit your meals out to once a week during the weight-loss phase of your diet. Once you move on to the maintenance plan, you can eat out more often.

- Read the whole menu before deciding what to order. The more courses you order, the fussier you need to be about each.
- Gravitate toward higher protein options. Shrimp, smoked salmon, calamari (not deep-fried) and tofu are great choices for entrees.
- Choose salads or soups for starters but avoid cream soups.
- Order dishes described as grilled, steamed, poached or stir-fried.
- Avoid dishes described as deep-fried, pan-fried, battered or crumbed.
- Avoid sauces with cheese, butter or cream. Dressings with a little olive oil and balsamic vinegar are fine.
- Just say no to french fries (steal one from someone else if you really need a taste).
- If the menu in the restaurant does not fit the Total Wellbeing Diet at all, order an appetizer-sized meal and extra steamed vegetables.
- If you can't resist a dessert, share one.
- Instead of a dessert, you could have a low-fat cappuccino or latte.

- Don't be afraid to ask how a meal is prepared, to ask for something different or to request the sauces and dressings "on the side."
- Beware of alcohol—it's a known saboteur of best intentions. Don't start drinking until your meal arrives, as alcohol can increase your appetite. Stick to 2 standard drinks (see page 61), go slowly and sip water in between.

**Marion** is a 60-year-old retired school teacher who despite regular exercise was considerably overweight. After 15 months on the Total Wellbeing Diet, she has lost 30 pounds and her blood cholesterol level has fallen from 215 mg/dL to 185 mg/dL. She is very happy with her overall weight loss, continues to exercise and follows the eating plan well. She has found the Diet easy to follow and hasn't felt hungry. She says the food and exercise checklists were very helpful in keeping her on track. These are her weight records over the course of the study.

| month | 0 | 1 | 2 | 3 | 6 | 9 | 12 | 15 |
|---|---|---|---|---|---|---|---|---|
| weight (lbs) | 201 | 192 | 184 | 180 | 168 | 165 | 165.5 | 171 |

**Sally** is a 53-year-old shop assistant who did no regular exercise other than while she was at her job. She had been watching her fat intake but she was still overweight at 175 pounds. After 15 months on the Total Wellbeing Diet she lost 29 pounds. She found it very easy to follow the Diet and she never felt hungry. Sally says she now has lots of energy.

| month | 0 | 1 | 2 | 3 | 6 | 9 | 12 | 15 |
|---|---|---|---|---|---|---|---|---|
| weight (lbs) | 175 | 168 | 163 | 157 | 147 | 141 | 139 | 146 |

**Fiona** is a 44-year-old clerk who exercises twice a week by swimming and walking for 30–45 minutes. She entered the trial at 263 pounds, which classed her as obese. She found the Diet very easy to follow, but also rates the regular checks as important to her success. After 15 months she is still overweight, but has managed to keep off most of the 27 pounds she has lost. Although her cholesterol, glucose and insulin levels were within the normal range to start with, they all improved as she lost weight.

| month | 0 | 1 | 2 | 3 | 6 | 9 | 12 | 15 |
|---|---|---|---|---|---|---|---|---|
| weight (lbs) | 263 | 247 | 238 | 229 | 222 | 227 | 237 | 236 |

**Kathy** is a 30-year-old housewife who weighed 240 pounds. She considered herself generally active and played netball once a week. She found the Total Wellbeing Diet easy and pleasant to follow and says the best thing for her was knowing what she had to eat each day. Kathy did find things a bit tough in the first 2 weeks, but found that after that the Diet became second nature. After 15 months on the Diet she has lost 65 pounds.

| month | 0 | 1 | 2 | 3 | 6 | 9 | 12 | 15 |
|---|---|---|---|---|---|---|---|---|
| weight (lbs) | 240 | 221 | 208 | 200 | 182 | 178 | 180 | 175 |

# energy balance & exercise

2

## changing your energy balance

Scientists use the term "energy" a little differently from the way it is commonly used. Energy is another word for calories in "nutrition-speak." For the rest of this chapter and throughout this book, we will refer to "calories" rather than "energy."

The basis of all effective weight-loss diets is calorie balance and control. In the short term, your total calorie intake has the greatest impact on your ability to lose weight, which is how the Total Wellbeing Diet works. This chapter shows you how you can calculate your daily calorie needs, minimize loss of muscle and maximize loss of fat by combining your diet with regular, moderate exercise.

- When the number of calories you eat in food and drink (intake) is equal to the number of calories you burn up (output), your weight will remain stable.
- When your calorie intake is greater than your calorie output, you will put on weight.
- To lose weight, your calorie intake must be less than your calorie output.

## calculating your calorie needs for weight loss

To understand your daily calorie needs, and what your intake needs to be to lose weight, you must estimate your daily calorie output. Your total daily calorie output is made up of three parts.

1   Resting metabolic rate—the calories required to maintain the body's systems at rest. This accounts for 60–80 percent of total daily calorie output in most inactive adults.

2   Thermic effect of food intake—the increase in calorie output above the resting metabolic rate that results when you eat, digest and store food throughout the day. This usually accounts for 6–10 percent of total daily calorie output.

3   Thermic effect of activity—includes the cost in calories of daily activities above the resting metabolic rate, such

as working (if you have a sedentary job), cooking, driving, cleaning, and planned exercise activities such as running, weight-training and walking. This accounts for 10–15 percent of the total calorie output in sedentary people, but is the most variable component of output and could account for as much as 50 percent in very active people.

You can calculate your total daily calorie output using equations to estimate resting metabolic rate, then multiply this by an appropriate activity factor.

Calculate your resting metabolic rate in calories using one of the following equations. You will need to know your height in inches, your weight in pounds, your age in years and your gender (that should be easy!).

**women**

655.1 + (4.35 x weight) + (4.7 x height) − (4.68 x age)

**men**

66.47 + (6.25 x weight) + (12.7 x height) − (6.76 x age)

*Example*

Susan is 32 years old, 62 inches tall and weighs 154 pounds. Her resting metabolic rate will be:

655.1 + (4.35 x 154) + (4.7 x 62) − (4.68 x 32)

= 655.1 + 669.9 + 291.4 − 149.76

= 1466.64 calories per day

Once you have calculated your resting metabolic rate, multiply it by an appropriate activity factor selected from the chart below to work out your total daily energy output.

**ACTIVITY FACTORS FOR ESTIMATING TOTAL ENERGY OUTPUT**

| activity level | description | activity factor |
|---|---|---|
| sedentary | little or no exercise, desk job | 1.2 |
| lightly active | light exercise or sports 1–3 days a week | 1.375 |
| moderately active | moderate exercise or sports 3–5 days a week | 1.55 |
| very active | hard exercise or sports 6–7 days a week | 1.725 |
| extremely active | hard daily exercise or sports or physical job or hard training (for marathon, triathlon etc.) | 1.9 |

So if Susan was relatively inactive, her total calorie output would be 1467 x 1.2 = 1760 calories per day, but if she was training for a marathon, her total output would be 1467 x 1.9 = 2787 calories per day.

## Adjusting your calorie intake for weight loss or maintenance

The total calorie output value you just calculated represents how many calories you need to take in each day in food and drink to keep your weight stable.

To lose weight, you need either to:
• reduce the number of calories you take in from food, or
• keep your calorie intake the same and increase your physical activity levels.

The safest and most effective way to reduce calorie intake for weight loss is to eat 500–1000 calories per day fewer than you use. This will produce a minimum weight loss of 1–2 pounds per week.

There is little evidence that faster weight loss or greater calorie restriction will improve long-term weight-loss outcomes. In our trials, we found that people on the Total Wellbeing Diet lost on average 17.5–20 pounds during the initial 12 weeks.

To calculate your recommended daily calorie intake for weight loss, subtract your daily calorie deficit from your total daily calorie output as follows.

### Example

Susan is relatively inactive, so she needs 1800 calories each day in order to maintain her current body weight. If she wants to lose 1 pound per week, then she needs a daily calorie deficit of 500 calories per day. Therefore her recommended daily calorie intake will be:

1800 – 500
= 1300 calories per day

## choosing the level to suit your daily calorie needs (if you want to!)

There are four plans or "Levels" designed to suit different daily calorie needs in the Total Wellbeing Diet. As a rule, Level 1 or 2 will be suitable for most women and Level 3 or 4 for most men, but it is best to calculate your own Level.

Once you have calculated your own recommended daily calorie intake for your weight-loss goals, choose the column or Level that is closest to your recommended intake from the table on page 30. If you find that you are losing weight too rapidly and feel too hungry on the Level you have chosen, try moving up a Level. Note that within each Level alcohol is an option. If you choose not to drink, you can replace 1 glass of wine with an extra indulgence food equal to 100 calories. Check the nutrition panel on the label of whatever food takes your fancy!

For Susan, the right level to follow is Level 1, the standard Total Wellbeing Diet plan. As a rule, women will lose weight on Level 1 or 2, while men will lose weight comfortably on Level 3 or 4.

Remember, any diet, including the Total Wellbeing Diet, should be combined with moderate exercise, to minimize loss of muscle and maximize loss of fat.

## CALORIE LEVELS FOR WEIGHT LOSS BASED ON RECOMMENDED DAILY ENERGY INTAKE

| Recommended daily energy intake (cal) | 1300 | 1400 | 1700 | 1900 |
|---|---|---|---|---|
| Level | 1 | 2 | 3 | 4 |
| dinner lean protein (oz/day) | 7 | 7 | 8 | 10 |
| lunch lean protein (oz/day) | 3.5* | 3.5* | 3.5* | 3.5* |
| whole grain bread (slices/day) | 2 | 2 | 2 | 2 |
| high-fiber cereal (g/day) | 40 | 40 | 50 | 50 |
| fruit (pieces/day) | 2 | 2 | 2 | 3 |
| low-fat dairy (servings/day) | 2 | 2 | 3 | 3 |
| vegetables from free list (cups/day) | 2 | 2 | 2 | 2 |
| salad (cups/day) | ½ | ½ | ½ | ½ |
| fats and oils (teaspoons/day) | 3 | 3 | 3 | 4 |
| low-calorie soup (optional) (ml/day) | 250 | 250 | 250 | 250 |
| wine (optional) (2×5 oz glasses/week)** | 2 | 2 | 2 | 2 |
| indulgence food*** (times/week) | 0 | 7 | 7 | 7 |

\* Or 1½ oz and 1 extra dairy serving
\*\* If you prefer not to drink, replace each glass of wine with one extra indulgence food of 100 calories
\*\*\* Equivalent to 100 calories, for example, 1 oz chocolate

# how exercise helps

Many people begin a serious exercise program with the expectation of losing large amounts of weight quickly.

There is a vast amount of evidence to show that exercise alone is not a very effective way to lose weight. If you are overweight or obese, reducing your calorie intake through dietary modification is a far more effective way to lose weight. But don't use this as a reason to do no exercise at all! In the long term, there are many benefits to be gained from regular exercise, both in terms of health and weight management. Exercise forms a perfect partnership with reduced calorie intake, because together they deliver the following great results.

- They maximize loss of fat and minimize loss of lean muscle.
- They assist in long-term maintenance and prevention of weight regain by increasing calorie output, using excess calories that would otherwise be stored as fat.

Here's why it's important to minimize loss of muscle. Your resting metabolic rate is largely determined by your lean muscle mass, because muscle requires a great deal of calories just to sustain it. When you lose weight through dieting alone, the weight comes from both fat and muscle. When you lose muscle, you reduce your metabolic rate, which is one reason it becomes progressively harder to sustain weight loss and maintain a steady body weight on a diet alone.

However, exercising regularly while you diet maximizes fat loss while preserving muscle. People who exercise have a higher metabolic rate, so their bodies burn more calories per minute, even when they're asleep. These extra calories used through a higher metabolic rate, combined with the increased calorie output from exercising, are important for successful long-term weight loss and for maintaining a stable body weight. Exercise is an essential part of any weight-loss program and it's also a great way to keep the weight off.

In fact, scientific evidence indicates that the combination of diet and exercise is the most effective approach for weight loss. We can't emphasize too much the benefits of keeping active for long-term weight maintenance.

## further health benefits of regular physical activity

Moderate regular physical activity provides a number of other health benefits, apart from weight maintenance. It:

- strengthens the heart, improves breathing and increases fitness levels
- improves flexibility and balance
- increases happiness and feelings of well-being
- increases energy
- reduces stress
- reduces blood pressure
- reduces blood cholesterol and triglyceride levels, and
- reduces the risk of a number of chronic diseases, including type 2 diabetes, heart disease, cancer, osteoporosis and arthritis.

And it's fun.

# your exercise program

Try to do at least 30 minutes of moderate-intensity physical activity daily. If possible, you should also include regular, vigorous aerobic exercise a few times a week. The benefits are greatest when you combine aerobic or cardiovascular exercise (walking, jogging, cycling, swimming, rowing, dancing) with resistance and flexibility training (yoga, Pilates, lifting weights, resistance exercises). Try to do resistance training at least twice a week.

## Initial health assessment

If you are over 50, have a medical condition or are pregnant, and you want to begin a vigorous training program, you should first undergo a stress test under medical supervision. If you simply want to walk, a stress test is probably not necessary. Check with your doctor.

## Daily incidental physical activity—it all counts!

You can find ways to increase your physical activity simply by thinking more about the way you live your life. Here are some great ideas for getting more active.

- Don't rely so much on your car. Instead, walk or cycle short distances and park your car further away from entrances to shops, movie theaters or work and walk the rest.
- Get off the bus, tram or train two or three stops earlier and walk the rest.
- Use the stairs whenever you can instead of the escalator or elevator. Even if you work in a high-rise building, you can probably get out of the elevator a couple of floors early and take the stairs for the rest.
- Play golf without a cart or caddy.

- Take advantage of any chance to be active throughout the day. Take a 10–20 minute walk at lunchtime or replace your coffee breaks with exercise breaks.
- Walk on a treadmill while you watch the news.
- During television commercials, walk up and down the stairs or jog on the spot.
- Remember that housework and gardening use up energy too. Clean the house a little every day. Not only will you expend more energy, but cleaning won't seem such a chore.

  Even if you can only manage to increase your physical activity in short bursts throughout the day, these still add up. If you only exercise for 5 minutes at a time, but do this six times a day, you've managed your daily 30 minutes of exercise. It's not the best way to exercise, but it's certainly better than doing nothing.

## Maintaining an exercise program

- Ask your family, friends or coworkers to start exercising with you. Exercise can be more enjoyable in groups of two or three. Making a commitment with someone else can also be a subtle form of motivation, and can help make you exercise regularly.
- Get into a routine. Set aside certain times of the day to exercise and don't permit outside factors like work, television or shopping to interfere. If the weather is bad, dance to your favorite music, work out at home or walk through your local shopping center. Once you have made a commitment to change, don't let poor excuses like the weather stop you.
- Set short- and long-term goals: aim to exercise for a certain amount of time and/or continue to exercise

until you reach a predetermined distance or number of repetitions.
- Keep an exercise diary so you can see the progress you have made.
- Choose a variety of physical activities to help you meet your goals, prevent boredom and keep your mind and body challenged.
- Wear comfortable clothes and shoes that are appropriate to the activity.
- Don't join a gym or buy expensive equipment if you can't afford to. Many types of exercise can be done at home or in the local community without spending any money.
- Make it easy for you to exercise. If you do join a gym, make sure it's close to home. Walk to the gym.

## Aerobic exercise for weight control

Exercise programs to reduce body fat or help maintain weight also improve the efficiency of the cardiovascular system. Each structured daily exercise session should be divided into three phases: warm-up, exercise and cool-down. The warm-up and cool-down are important components of the exercise session, helping to prevent muscle soreness or injuries.

### 1   Warm-up (5–10 minutes)

Warm-up the muscles you will be using in your exercise session. Begin with gentle stretching exercises, followed by 5–10 minutes of low-intensity activity using the mode of exercise you are about to engage in. For example, if you are going for a jog, stretch your leg muscles first, then jog at a slower than normal pace for several minutes.

2   Exercise training (20–45 minutes)

This is the most important phase of your structured exercise session, in which you perform actual aerobic exercise. It is during this phase that you will attain the health and weight-control benefits of the exercise.

3   Cool-down (5–10 minutes)

Every structured exercise session should conclude with a cool-down period, to help return the cardiovascular system to normal. This is best achieved by gradually slowing your exercise pace down during the last several minutes of your workout. This will help keep the blood flowing back to the heart and prevent blood pooling in the exercised muscles. If you stop exercising abruptly, blood can pool in the legs, making you dizzy and light-headed. Complete the cool-down by stretching; this may help prevent muscle stiffness and improve flexibility.

## Resistance and flexibility training

Regular resistance training can really help maintain muscle strength and endurance. By preserving muscle, you are helping your body burn more calories, which will make weight loss easier. Resistance training can also help reshape your body by improving muscle tone, and has a beneficial effect on your blood sugar levels.

You don't need to go to the gym to do resistance training; try doing simple exercises at home like push-ups, pull-ups, sit-ups and squats. And cans of food make great impromptu weights for improving upper body strength!

# eating for lifelong health & well-being

The Total Wellbeing Diet is not just about weight loss. It's about total well-being. That's why it includes all food groups, to ensure you eat the right balance of protein foods, cereal grains, dairy foods, fruits and vegetables to maximize your micronutrient intake for lifelong health and vitality. It's also a sustainable and flexible eating plan that you'll find you can follow long term because it's easy to adapt as your calorie needs change. The daily menus we have created focus on nutrient density and provide you with such a wide variety of foods to choose from that they may change the way you think about healthy eating and losing weight forever.

This chapter tells you about the nutrient-rich foods you'll be eating every day. You may already be familiar with the five food groups. The Total Wellbeing Diet includes each of those important food groups, but in different proportions. Here, we take a closer look at each of these groups and the essential nutrients that these foods give us, and we show you how we have built them into our menu plans. We also include shopping tips to help you make the right choices.

The five food groups you will be eating are as follows.

1   Lean red meat, chicken, fish and alternatives such as eggs, legumes, whole grains, nuts and seeds

2   Milk and milk products, including yogurt and cheese

3   Fruits and vegetables

4   Breads and cereals

5   Fats and oils

When you approach food by thinking about what you *should* be eating each day, rather than what you can't have, you will feel more positive about your diet and not need to resort to unplanned snacking. Our volunteers found that this way of thinking helped keep them on track.

## NUTRIENTS IN TOTAL WELLBEING DIET

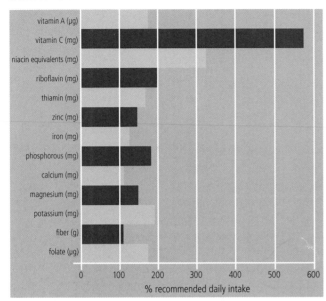

% recommended daily intake

# red meat, chicken, fish and alternatives

Foods in this nutrient-rich group (red meat, chicken, fish, and alternatives such as eggs) play an essential role in a healthy, balanced diet. They provide us with all-important protein (as do dairy products), along with numerous vitamins and minerals, including iron and zinc, vitamin B12, and those essential omega-3s.

## Protein—creating, maintaining and renewing your body cells

To grow and develop you need protein. This vital nutrient helps to create, maintain and renew the tissues in your body. In fact, every living cell, fluid or process in your body contains or needs proteins. Enzymes and some hormones such as insulin are proteins and play vital roles in the body's day-to-day processes. Your muscles and vital organs are made up of protein. Proteins are also important in making antibodies, which help you fight infection and disease.

The building blocks of protein are amino acids. Your body makes some of these amino acids itself. Others, called "essential amino acids," you have to get from the food you eat because your body can't make them.

There are plenty of protein-rich foods to choose from. Some come from animal sources (red meat, chicken, fish, eggs and dairy foods) and are what we call "complete proteins" because they supply all the essential amino acids.

Apart from soy products (including tofu), which are also complete proteins, plant proteins are called "incomplete" because they don't supply all the essential amino acids. However, foods like legumes (beans, split peas, lentils and chickpeas), nuts and seeds plus whole grains can give you all the essential amino acids you need provided you eat a wide variety of them each day.

If you are deriving much of your daily protein intake from plant sources, remember that they contain a lower proportion of protein than animal sources. Grains and legumes also contain carbohydrates, and nuts are high in (albeit healthy) fats, which you need to keep in mind in light of the daily allowances on the Total Wellbeing Diet.

Sources of protein include the following.

Animal sources
- Lean red meat, including beef, veal and lamb
- Lean white meat, including pork and skinless chicken

- Fish and shellfish
- Low-fat dairy products, including cottage cheese, yogurt and milk
- Eggs

Plant sources
- Legumes, including beans, split peas, lentils and chickpeas
- Tofu and other soy products
- Nuts and seeds
- Whole grains

As we have explained, the Total Wellbeing Diet is a protein-plus eating plan. When you're on it, you'll find that you're eating around 10 oz of lean protein foods a day, which will help you feel satisfied for longer, help control your blood fats and, most important, supply you with many essential nutrients for health and vitality.

The volunteers who took part in the Total Wellbeing Diet trials obtained most of their protein from the red meat/fish/chicken and dairy groups. We don't yet know whether vegetable protein sources are as effective in the Diet as animal protein sources, but if you are vegetarian and you want to try a higher protein pattern, we can give you suggestions for how to modify it. If dairy foods and eggs are part of your diet, you shouldn't have any problem achieving our protein intake. We suggest you substitute 3.5 oz tofu or 4 oz cooked beans or lentils for 3.5 oz lean red meat, chicken or fish. However, achieving our recommended protein intake on a vegan diet could be a challenge without going overboard on carbohydrates or fat. We recommend that you discuss appropriate exchanges with an accredited dietitian.

Our bodies have evolved to thrive on a wide variety of both animal and plant foods. Many people eat a plant-based diet by way of necessity, but others choose to for a wide range of reasons. Population studies have shown that vegetarians have a lower risk of obesity, coronary heart disease, high blood pressure, type 2 diabetes and some forms of cancer—but it is not clear if this is due to their diet or their lifestyle. However, if you are a vegetarian, you need to plan your diet carefully to make sure that all essential nutrients are included.

**TYPES OF VEGETARIAN DIETS**

| vegetarian type | animal products avoided | animal products eaten |
| --- | --- | --- |
| lacto- | red meat, fish, poultry, eggs | milk, milk products |
| lacto-ovo- | red meat, fish, poultry | eggs, egg products, milk, milk products |
| pesco- | red meat, poultry | fish, eggs, egg products, milk, milk products |
| vegan | all | none |

## Just one day for vegetarians

### Breakfast
1½ oz high-fiber breakfast cereal (e.g., Raisin Bran) with 8 oz low-fat milk

1 sliced banana

Breakfast = 1 unit cereal, 1 unit dairy, 1 unit fruit

### Lunch
Egg and salad sandwich (2 slices whole grain bread with 2 teaspoons light margarine, 2 eggs and ½ cup salad leaves)

1 apple

Lunch = 2 units bread, 1 unit protein, 1 unit fats, 1 unit fruit, ½ unit veggies

## Dinner

7 oz tofu with 2 cups stir-fried vegetables (cooked with 2 teaspoons oil and flavored with ingredients from the free list on page 23)

8 oz low-fat yogurt

Dinner = 2 units protein, 2 units fats, 2 units veggies, 1 unit dairy

## Iron—giving you energy

Iron is an essential mineral in your diet. You need it to form hemoglobin, which helps transport oxygen to every part of your body. Iron deficiency, the most common nutrient deficiency in the world, leads to tiredness, lack of energy and poor stamina. It's a common problem for women of reproductive age. Women need much more iron than men (about twice as much) due to blood loss through menstruation and the demands of a developing baby during pregnancy. On top of this, many women do not obtain the recommended daily amounts of iron for a variety of reasons—they don't eat much red meat, they skip meals and they go on very restrictive diets that eliminate whole food groups. Vegetarians can also be at risk of iron deficiency. However, legumes, leafy greens, iron-enriched products (such as cereals), brewer's yeast and dried fruits are all useful plant sources of iron, especially when combined with vitamin C–rich foods.

There are two types of iron—heme iron (from animal sources) and non-heme iron from plant sources. Your body can absorb heme iron much more readily than non-heme iron. So although certain plant foods contain significant amounts of iron, the amount your body absorbs is only 2–5 percent of it. On the other hand, your body will absorb 15–25 percent of iron from an animal source.

The good news is that some foods (red meat and vitamin C–rich foods) promote the absorption of iron from plant foods when you eat or drink them at the same time. That's why a glass of orange juice with your breakfast cereal can better help you absorb the iron in your cereal.

It's also important to keep in mind that the caffeine in your coffee or cocoa, the tannin in your tea, phytates in bran and whole grains, fiber, and oxalates (in green leafy vegetables) inhibit the absorption of iron from grains. This is because they bind and hold iron so that your body can't absorb it properly.

And in case you needed to know, Popeye got it wrong about spinach. Although spinach contains a lot of iron, it's non-heme iron (not well absorbed) and is packed with natural fiber and phytates that bind most of the iron so your body can't absorb it if it is eaten alone.

Good sources of iron include the following.

Heme iron
- Lean red meat, chicken, fish and seafood are good sources of heme iron. The best are lean red meat, liver, kidney and heart, which have around twice as much iron as chicken and three times as much as fish. Oysters are a good source.

Non-heme iron
- Legumes (beans, lentils, chickpeas)
- Eggs (the yolk)
- Cereal grains, whole grain and whole meal breads, iron-fortified breakfast cereals
- Dark green leafy vegetables, including cabbage, broccoli
- Dried fruits
- Nuts and seeds

## Zinc—life would not be the same without it

Zinc plays a crucial role in growth and cell division, where it is required for DNA and protein synthesis (important in the building and repair of muscle and tissue, which is why zinc helps cuts and wounds heal). It's a component of many enzymes, which is why you need it for carbohydrate and protein metabolism. Zinc also helps us fight infections, as it is essential for a strong immune system—have you noticed how many cold and flu preparations contain zinc? Life would simply not be the same without zinc, as it is vital for your ability to taste, smell and see. Men need more than women because male semen contains 100 times more zinc than is found in the blood. The more sexually active a man, the more zinc he needs to produce healthy sperm.

As with iron, the adequacy of dietary zinc depends not only on your overall intake, but on how much you actually absorb. Animal sources of zinc enhance absorption. Phytic acid, however, found in plant sources such as whole grains, legumes and some other vegetables, is an inhibitor.

The best sources for zinc are as follows.

Animal sources
- Lean red meat
- Lean white meat
- Fish and seafood (oysters are the richest by far—10 times greater than lean red meat, which is number 2)
- Dairy foods
- Eggs

Plant sources
- Legumes
- Nuts (particularly cashews and peanuts) and seeds (pumpkin seeds provide one of the most concentrated food sources of zinc, which is useful for vegetarians)
- Whole grains (the outer husk of cereal whole grains contains zinc, but it's lost when those products are refined)

## Omega-3—one of the "good" fats of life

Omega-3 fatty acids are essential to healthy growth and development, playing a vital role in every cell, tissue and organ in your body. For example in the heart, the cells are more regulated and beat on time when you have enough omega-3s. They are useful in the treatment of conditions such as rheumatoid arthritis and can protect the body against heart disease. In fact, trials in people with heart disease have shown that long-chain omega-3 fats from fish oil can reduce sudden death from heart attack by about 45 percent.

There are two types of omega-3s.
- Short-chain omega-3 fatty acids (alpha-linolenic acid or ALA) come from plant sources, such as green leafy vegetables, canola oil, linseed oil, soybean oil and mustard seed oil.
- Long-chain omega-3 fatty acids (eicosapentaenoic acid or EPA and docosahexaenoic acid or DHA) come from fish and seafood, especially oily fish, such as sardines, ocean trout, Atlantic salmon, smoked salmon, canned salmon, Alaskan salmon, fresh tuna, canned mackerel, mullet, herring, cod, bluefish and calamari.

As your body doesn't produce omega-3s, it relies on the food you eat to obtain them. The omega-3 fatty acids derived from fish are much more potent than those from plant sources, which is why we recommend that you eat fish twice a week on the Total Wellbeing Diet. Oily fish will give your omega-3s a real boost. White fish have much smaller amounts of omega-3s, but they will help you reduce the total amount of fat in your diet. In fact, eating fish of any kind, even in small amounts, reduces your risk of heart disease.

## Vitamin B12

We need vitamin B12 for strong, healthy blood cells and for DNA repair and maintenance. Deficiency can lead to a form of anemia called pernicious anemia, which can cause nerve damage. Although this is usually the result of an inability to absorb B12, it can also be caused by a dietary deficiency.

We don't need very much B12—the recommended daily allowance is just 2.4 mcg. However, this important vitamin isn't found in many foods. Lean red meat is a good source—a lean 3.5 oz steak contains 2.4 mcg. Other sources include dairy foods. As there are no plant sources of B12, vegans may need to consider taking a supplement.

## Choosing your protein foods

On the Total Wellbeing Diet you will be eating 2 units (7 oz raw weight) of lean red meat (beef, lamb or veal) for dinner 4 times each week. We recommend 2 units fish for dinner twice a week, and 2 units fat-trimmed, skinless chicken or other protein food for dinner one night a week. For lunch you will be taking your pick from one 3.5 oz (raw weight) unit of any lean protein source (canned or fresh fish or seafood, chicken, pork, ham, beef, lamb or turkey) each day. You can replace this 3.5 oz lean protein unit with 2 eggs or an extra unit from the dairy group any time.

Here's how to shop wisely on the protein-plus Diet.

### • Lean red meat

Choose lean cuts of red meats (beef, veal and lamb) whenever possible. They are widely available. Check out the difference in fat content between some untrimmed and lean meats in this table.

**FAT CONTENT OF LEAN AND UNTRIMMED MEATS**

| meat | lean (g fat/3.5 oz meat) | untrimmed (g fat/3.5 oz meat) |
|---|---|---|
| rump steak | 5 | 10 |
| minced beef | 7 | 10 |
| roast leg lamb | 6 | 12 |
| roast leg pork or pork chops | 4 | 27 |

Removing the visible fat on meat reduces your saturated fat intake, which is beneficial for your heart.

Reduced-fat varieties of sausages and cold cuts are also good choices. When shopping for processed meat, look for fat content below 10 percent and reduced salt content.

Cheaper cuts of meat are just as nutritious as more expensive cuts, but they are more tender and tastier when prepared in dishes that are cooked more slowly, such as casseroles, stews and pot roasts. Again, remember to trim off the fat first, or ask your butcher to do it for you.

## • Chicken and pork

Chicken contains similar amounts of protein to red meat and with the skin removed is low in fat—1 oz per 3.5 oz without skin for breast meat and .5 oz per 3.5 oz with skin. The same applies to turkey, but duck is considerably higher in fat. Lean pork is also low in fat (see table on page 42).

## • Fish and seafood

Fish and seafood contain similar amounts of protein to lean meat and are often low in fat—$^1/_{10}$–$^1/_3$ oz per 3.5 oz. Fish tends to be higher in polyunsaturated fats than the meat of most land animals. But higher-fat fish are an excellent source of long-chain omega-3 fats, so don't panic about the fat content of fish flesh!

**FAT CONTENT OF FISH AND SEAFOOD**

| fish or seafood category | examples | fat | cholesterol | omega-3s |
|---|---|---|---|---|
| mollusks | mussels, oysters, squid | low | low | moderate |
| crustaceans | shrimp, crabs, lobster | low | high | moderate |
| white fish | whiting, perch, mako, flake, flounder | low | low | moderate |
| oily fish | sardines (in oil), ocean trout, Atlantic salmon, tuna, herring, mackerel | high | moderate | high |

Some people worry about mercury levels in fish, but the amounts recommended in the Total Wellbeing Diet are well within the guidelines for safe consumption.

## • Eggs

Eggs are an excellent low-fat source of protein, vitamins and minerals. Brown eggs are very popular, but in fact the color of the shell does not affect the flavor or nutrient value of an egg. The yolk, however, is affected by what the hen eats, so hens raised on corn, clover or grass may produce yolks of a richer orange. You can also buy "omega-enriched" eggs. This simply means that the hens have been fed either canola meal or linseeds or sometimes fishmeal. The cholesterol and total fat of these eggs remain the same.

The cholesterol content of eggs has often been given as a reason to avoid eggs in order to control blood cholesterol levels. But eggs on average contribute only about a quarter of the cholesterol in our daily diet. You need to know the following about eggs and cholesterol.

- It is safe for most people with normal blood cholesterol levels not to restrict their intake of eggs. In the Total Wellbeing Diet, you can use 2 eggs as a replacement for 3.5 oz protein food at lunchtime.
- People with very high blood cholesterol should restrict their egg consumption to up to 4 a week. The Total Wellbeing Diet is low in saturated fat, which will reduce your blood cholesterol, as will your weight loss.
- The fat and cholesterol in an egg are confined to the yolk. An average egg contains 190 mg cholesterol.

## milk and milk products, including yogurt and cheese

Low-fat dairy foods not only provide complete protein, they are the best source of calcium for your body. They also provide numerous essential minerals and vitamins, including vitamin A and riboflavin (vitamin B2). Over the years, 2–3 units of low-fat dairy foods a day has been a simple and enduring nutrition message for bone health. Yet one in two American women over

50 and one in four men over 50 experiences a fracture due to osteoporosis. In 2004, nearly 10 million Americans had osteoporosis, and almost 34 million more are estimated to have low bone mass, placing them at increased risk for osteoporosis.

Why? Well, we are frequently told by our volunteers that dairy foods are "the first to go" as a way to limit fat intake when people go on a weight-loss diet. Limiting foods such as butter, cream and cheese can certainly significantly reduce your calorie intake without affecting the actual volume of food you eat. However, totally avoiding dairy foods is not only unnecessary, it's unwise.

Dairy foods can be a part of any weight-loss diet, as there are many reduced-fat (and even nonfat) dairy products available. Surveys of thousands of people in the United States in the 1980s as well as more recently have found that those with higher intakes of calcium and dairy foods also had lower body weight and less body fat. This doesn't mean that dairy foods are intrinsically slimming, but it does suggest that these protein foods are satisfying.

It's important to remember that just eating fat does not make you overweight. Your body weight reflects the balance between your total calorie intake (from carbohydrates, fats, protein and alcohol) and calorie output (see Chapter 2). On pages 56–57 we show you why not all fats are bad.

### Boning up on calcium

Calcium is the main mineral component of your bones, teeth and nails. It also has many other important functions that are essential to keeping us alive—muscle contraction and regulation of the heartbeat, for example. If your diet doesn't supply enough calcium for these processes, your body will immediately draw on its backup supply—your skeleton, which contains about 2 pounds of calcium! This is because bone is easily broken down to release calcium into the bloodstream and ensure that your heart muscle keeps beating. But bone will eventually lose density if this continues long term.

Good sources of calcium are as follows.

Animal sources
- Milk
- Yogurt
- Cheese
- Ice cream and dairy desserts
- Canned salmon and sardines (including the small edible bones)
- Shrimp

Plant sources
- Whole grain cereals and breads
- Legumes
- Tofu
- Soy drinks (fortified)
- Sesame seeds
- Nuts (particularly almonds, Brazil nuts and hazelnuts)
- Dried figs
- Spinach and broccoli

As with iron, not all the calcium in food is absorbed—some passes straight through your digestive system. Depending on the food, the proportion of calcium that your body can absorb varies. Dairy foods contain additional components that enhance calcium absorption. For example, we can absorb more calcium from an 8 oz glass of low-fat milk (102 calories) than from a 4 oz serving of almonds (638 calories), even though both contain about 280 mg of calcium.

One unit of dairy food contains about 300 mg calcium and is equal to:
- an 8 oz container of yogurt
- 8 oz milk
- 3.5 oz canned salmon (with bones), or
- 1 oz hard cheese (matchbox-sized).

The recommended daily calcium intake for adults depends on a number of factors including your age, whether you are male or female, pregnant, breast-feeding or menopausal. The recommended daily dietary intake of calcium in the following table from the National Institutes of Health is designed to cover the needs of most people.

**RECOMMENDED CALCIUM INTAKE PER DAY**

| category | recommended daily intake (mg) |
|---|---|
| INFANTS<br>birth–6 months<br>6–12 months | 400<br>600 |
| CHILDREN<br>1–5 years<br>6–10 years | 800<br>800–1200 |
| ADOLESCENTS AND YOUNG ADULTS*<br>11–24 years | 1200–1500 |
| WOMEN<br>25–50 years | 1000 |
| PREGNANT OR LACTATING WOMEN | 1500 |
| POSTMENOPAUSAL<br>taking HRT<br>not taking HRT* | 1000<br>1500 |
| MEN<br>25–65 years | 1000 |
| WOMEN AND MEN OVER 65* | 1500 |

* These groups should follow the three units dairy option of the Total Wellbeing Diet: replace 3.5 oz protein for lunch with 1.5 oz protein plus 1 extra dairy serving.

## Bones and osteoporosis

We tend to think of bone as static—just a solid framework to give our body support. In fact, bone is a highly active tissue made up of an internal honeycomblike structure with a hard outer covering. In the same way that skin continually sheds and grows new layers, bone also undergoes a continuous process of breakdown and regeneration, referred to as "remodeling." In childhood, we gain bone mass and grow taller because the regeneration process dominates over breakdown. Between 25 and 40, the two processes are in balance, so there is little change in bone mass. After the age of 40, however, breakdown slightly outweighs regrowth and we gradually lose bone. The honeycomb structure becomes more porous and the outer layer thins, reducing overall bone strength. Weaker bones are more susceptible to fractures. Bone loss happens equally in men and women, but it progresses at an accelerated rate during the first five years after menopause, due to a reduction in estrogen.

While this aging process cannot be prevented, much can be done to maximize how much bone we have in our later years. If we start with more bone, it stands to reason that more will be left after age-related bone loss. The most important contributor to bone mass is our genes. If our parents have good bone mass then we are more likely to. However, adequate daily dietary calcium and regular weight-bearing exercise are vital to achieving peak bone density in our mid-twenties, and to minimizing bone loss later on. Other lifestyle factors also influence bone health, such as cigarette smoking and an excessive intake of alcohol, caffeine or salt. For each gram of calcium we ingest, our bone mass increases by 1.4 percent, but 10 years of smoking a pack a day reduces bone density by 2.3–3.3 percent. Some studies show that high-protein foods can be associated with improved bone health. Because dairy foods are excellent sources of both calcium and protein, that makes them a must for keeping our bones healthy.

The Total Wellbeing Diet has been designed so that you achieve your calcium intake needs—reduced-fat milk with your cereal in the morning, a container of yogurt as a between-meal snack, canned fish or low-fat cheese in a sandwich at lunch.

Vegetarians absorb and retain more calcium than do non-vegetarians. Vegetable greens such as spinach and broccoli, and some legumes and soybean products are good sources of calcium. Vegetarians who eat dairy foods will obtain sufficient calcium.

## Choosing your dairy foods

On the Total Wellbeing Diet basic plan you will be having at least 2 units of dairy foods a day. One unit is equal to: 8 oz low-fat milk, 8 oz low-fat or diet yogurt (plain or flavored), 8 oz low-fat custard or dairy dessert, 1 oz cheddar cheese or other full-fat cheese, or 2 oz reduced-fat cheese (less than 10 percent fat). Adolescents and young adults, postmenopausal women not taking HRT, and women and men over 65 should follow the three units dairy option of the Total Wellbeing Diet, which replaces the 3.5 oz protein requirement at lunch with 1.5 oz protein plus 1 extra dairy unit.

# fruits and vegetables

Fruits and vegetables bring variety in flavor, texture, color and appearance to your meals and snacks. Not only that, they are bulky and satisfying without adding a lot of calories. As a group they make an extremely valuable contribution to your diet because they are low in fat, rich in fiber, an important source of folate and packed with nutrients including vitamin C, and a range of protective antioxidants including the colorful carotenoids.

Although we all know that fruit and vegetables are good for us, we actually have very little scientific information about why this is so. What we do know is that when scientists have looked at disease patterns and diet among different groups of people, they have found that where people eat more fruit and vegetables, the prevalence of heart disease and cancer is lower.

## Vitamin C

Vitamin C or ascorbic acid is vital for the formation of collagen (which helps make your skin smooth and firm), bones, teeth and healthy gums. It also helps your body resist infection and, as we mentioned earlier, assists in the absorption of iron from food. Historically vitamin C (from lime juice, citrus fruit and fresh vegetables when possible) was important in the prevention of scurvy—the curse of long sea voyages.

Because we excrete vitamin C in urine, we need to eat fruit and vegetables every day to keep our levels up. However, there's very little scientific evidence for taking megadoses to cure a cold, simply because the body gets rid of what it doesn't need. So there's little risk of overdosing on vitamin C—the body protects itself by efficiently excreting the excess in urine.

**THE RICHEST SOURCES OF VITAMIN C**

| food | vitamin C content (mg/100 g) |
| --- | --- |
| guava | 243 |
| black currants | 150–230 |
| peppers | 60–170 |
| strawberries | 40–90 |
| kiwifruit | 74 |
| papaya | 60 |
| lemons | 40–60 |
| oranges | 40–60 |
| cabbage—raw | 40–70 |
| cabbage—boiled | 10–40 |
| Brussels sprouts | 30–90 |
| cauliflower—boiled | 15–40 |
| broccoli—boiled | 15–40 |
| tomatoes | 10–30 |
| liver | 8–13 |
| kidney | 8–13 |
| potatoes | 4–14 |
| cow's milk | 4 |

## Folate (folic acid)

You need folate (which works in conjunction with vitamin B12) to produce and maintain red blood cells, for protein metabolism and for the formation of your DNA. It's also important in the pathway that controls the coordinated switching on and off of genes—vital during periods of rapid cell division and growth, such as infancy and pregnancy. Research has shown that it may be useful in preventing neural tube defects such as spina bifida and anencephaly in newborn babies. It may also reduce risk of heart disease (because it lowers homocysteine levels which are thought to be a risk factor) and cancer (by contributing to DNA synthesis and repair).

The recommended daily intake of folate for adults is 400 mcg; pregnant and breast-feeding women need more, about 600 mcg.

Good sources of folate include the following.

- Vegetables, particularly green leafy vegetables
- Fruits, including bananas, berries, apricots, melons and oranges
- Legumes, including chickpeas, lentils and dried beans, and peas
- Nuts and seeds, including peanuts, almonds and sunflower seeds
- Whole grain foods, including wheat germ, wheat bran, breads and fortified breakfast cereals
- Organ meats, such as liver and kidney

## Antioxidants—protecting your cells against damage

Antioxidants, including vitamins A, C and E, and the yellow-orange carotenoids, help counter the detrimental effects of "oxygen free radicals" (short-lived, highly active, destructive chemicals) that form naturally during food metabolism, and by external factors such as X-rays, ultraviolet radiation and pollution. Free radicals have been implicated in the development of several diseases, including cancer and heart disease, highlighting the need to consider our antioxidant levels as a key part of preventative medicine.

Research indicates that antioxidants inhibit cancer and heart disease, may block formation of cancer-producing chemicals in the stomach, and perhaps reduce the risk of colon cancer. In fact, it's estimated that the risk of cancer and heart disease is lower in people who consume 5–7 servings of antioxidant-rich fruits and vegetables a day. Studies also suggest that diets high in antioxidant-rich foods provide significant protection against degenerative conditions such as Alzheimer's disease.

However, as we still don't know exactly which antioxidants work, how, and in what combinations, the best advice we can give you is to eat a wide variety of fruits and vegetables every day.

There are a number of naturally occurring substances in food, such as vitamins and phenolic compounds, that have antioxidant properties.

### • Plant phenolics

The term "plant phenolics" includes a wide variety of naturally occurring compounds. Tea, coffee, and red and black berries are rich in simple or complex phenols (or polyphenols). The colors of most flowers and fruits are due to polyphenols. These substances have important antioxidant properties—that is, they can scavenge naturally occurring free radicals before they can damage fat, proteins or DNA. Polyphenols can also make arteries behave normally, allowing them to produce more relaxant chemicals.

### • Carotenoids

Carotenoids are pigments found in a variety of red, orange and yellow fruits and vegetables as well as some dark green leafy vegetables (such as spinach, cabbage and Brussels sprouts). The best known of these is beta-carotene. Like many carotenoids, beta-carotene is a powerful antioxidant (for example, it provides protection for the algae from which it is commercially harvested against harmful ultraviolet radiation from the sun).

It is also a precursor of vitamin A and retinoic acid, which can make cancer cells behave more like normal cells. The carotenoid lycopene (to which tomatoes owe their red color) is a very powerful antioxidant and has been associated with reduced risk of prostate cancer.

### • Isothiocyanates

The cruciferous vegetables—broccoli, cauliflower, cabbage, Brussels sprouts, bok choy, kale—contain many chemicals that have been linked to lower cancer risk, including glucosinolates, crambene, indole-3-carbinol and especially isothiocyanates (which are formed from glucosinolates). Cruciferous vegetables have been associated with protection from lung, stomach, bowel, bladder and prostate cancer.

## Choosing fruits and vegetables

On the Total Wellbeing Diet you'll be eating a wide variety of fruits and vegetables every day.

Enjoy 2 pieces (2 units) of fruit a day—fresh, frozen or canned unsweetened fruit. One unit is equivalent to 5 oz or $^2/_3$ cup unsweetened juice. There are plenty of fruits to choose from and to suit all tastes, so your snacks need never get boring. Try apples, apricots, bananas, blackberries, blueberries, cantaloupes, cherries, figs, grapes, guava, kiwifruit, mandarins, mangoes, nectarines, passionfruit, papaya, peaches, pears, pineapple, plums, oranges, raspberries, strawberries or watermelon.

Apart from potatoes, sweet potatoes and yams, vegetables contain very little carbohydrate and you can think of them as "free foods." The same goes for herbs and spices—a great way to bring flavor and variety to your meals. The Diet recommends eating 2½ cups of vegetables a day, which is equal to 5 standard servings. This 2½ cups is only a rough guide—some vegetables will be easy to measure in this way, such as peas, whereas others will be more difficult, such as lettuce. If you like to be meticulous, you can weigh them: 1 cup is equal to about 5 oz. There is no need to be obsessional about quantities of vegetables, however—if you have more it

should not be a major problem, as they contribute few extra calories but pack a lot of nutrients.

The following vegetables are permitted in the Total Wellbeing Diet: artichokes, asparagus, bean sprouts, beets, bok choy and Asian greens, broccoli, Brussels sprouts, carrots, cauliflower, celery, chili peppers, chives, corn, cucumber, fennel, green beans, lettuces and salad vegetables such as arugula and watercress, mushrooms, onions, parsnips, peas, pumpkin, radishes, red pepper, rutabagas, spinach, squash, Swiss chard, tomatoes, turnips and zucchini.

We are often asked whether or not it's better to buy organic produce. Although organic fruits and vegetables are probably no more nutritious than conventionally grown varieties, they may taste better. Some organic leafy vegetables and potatoes also seem to have higher vitamin C contents, which may be due to the fact that organic produce is often smaller and therefore denser than conventional produce, which has a high water content. The bottom line is that eating more fruits and vegetables, whether organic, conventional, fresh, frozen or canned, will increase your intake of protective compounds and is important for good health.

## breads and cereals

The Total Wellbeing Diet is lower in carbohydrate than some diets, but it is not a very low-carb diet—in fact it contains moderate amounts of carbohydrate foods, providing around 40 percent of your total daily calorie needs.

Carbohydrates (sugars and starches) are found mainly in plant foods such as cereal grains and products manufactured from them, such as pasta, breakfast cereal and bread, in vegetables and fruits, and in legumes such as

### Cooking and nutrients

Because some vitamins are water soluble and sensitive to heat and air, you need to take care handling fruits and vegetables when preparing meals. Choose fresh and undamaged food, slice in large pieces and use the least amount of water possible for cooking to retain the nutrients. Forget the old wives' tale about using baking soda when cooking green vegetables. Don't. It will increase the loss of vitamin C. Avoid copper utensils too—copper helps destroy vitamin C. Whether making salads or cooking vegetables and fruits, serve and eat meals and snacks as soon as possible after they are prepared, to ensure you get the benefits of the nutrients they provide. Vegetables lose 50 percent of their nutrients when boiled, but only 15 percent or less of their nutrients when steamed.

Cutting, shredding, homogenizing and juicing can expose many plant chemicals to oxygen in the air, which dramatically decreases the antioxidant levels. Many juice manufacturers are aware of this problem, however, and fortify their product (adding vitamin C, for example)—so bought juices can be just as good a source of vitamin C as the ones you make at home.

beans, peas and lentils. These are powerful fuel foods that keep you going.

When you eat a carbohydrate food, the sugars and starches are broken down in the stomach and small intestine to glucose, which is absorbed and then distributed to the body to provide energy for your muscles and the preferred fuel for your brain. While your body can make glucose from some amino acids in protein foods to meet direct needs, a lack of dietary carbohydrate leads to depletion of the body's glucose stores and eventually to poor physical and mental endurance. In addition to providing fuel, carbohydrate foods are often good sources of dietary fiber to keep your digestive system healthy and regular, and provide vital vitamins and minerals.

Despite the myths, carbohydrate foods are not intrinsically fattening. Although many weight-loss diets leave out carbohydrates altogether, this is unnecessary. No one food type is fattening on its own—it is the total amount of food eaten that counts. The problem can be that very refined carbohydrate foods often taste good, so many people tend to eat too much of them. (The same can be said of fatty foods.) Conversely, eating whole grain carbohydrates is associated with lower obesity risk—so not all carbohydrates are the same, and it is important to understand the difference!

In fact, less refined, carbohydrate-rich foods, such as whole grain breads and cereals, are critical in a balanced diet for weight reduction and maintenance. Not only that, people with diets high in whole grain products are much less likely to suffer from coronary heart disease, cancers and type 2 diabetes. Some of this protection may be due to lower body weight, since people who consume more whole grain foods are less overweight than the general population, or to the higher dietary fiber content of whole grains. However, it may be due to other major constituents of whole grains, such as protein and starch; important essential micronutrients, such as B-group vitamins; and antioxidants, which are more abundant in whole grain foods.

To extract the best value from the Total Wellbeing Diet, it's important to appreciate the contribution of whole grain breads and cereals. Grains have been dietary staples for millennia, and for most of recorded history they have been eaten in relatively unrefined form. Some cereals, such as oats in porridge and rye in crispbreads, are still consumed largely as whole grain foods, but other cereals, such as wheat and rice, are eaten as processed products. When grains are milled to separate the edible portion from the indigestible seed coat (bran), the result is a flour that is high in starch but that contains relatively few of the nutrients found in the bran and germ. The Total Wellbeing Diet includes controlled amounts of the less refined carbohydrates, such as whole grain breads and cereals, in the menus and recipes that we have developed.

Good sources of carbohydrate are as follows.

- Whole grain breads or fruit loaf
- High-fiber breakfast cereals
- Whole grain cereals, including barley, oats, rye, and couscous
- Legumes, including beans, peas and lentils
- Fruits, such as apples, bananas, oranges and dried fruits
- Dairy foods, including low-fat milk, ice cream and yogurt (not cheese).

## Keeping regular with dietary fiber

It's important to ensure that you get an adequate intake of dietary fiber, which in American diets comes mostly from whole grain cereal foods and fiber-rich cereal products. Some fiber also comes from legumes, vegetables and fruits. Eating a range of fiber-containing foods is what seems to deliver the maximum benefit.

Fiber promotes the optimal health and functioning of your gastro-intestinal system. It consists almost entirely of indigestible carbohydrates, all of which are resistant to digestion by human enzymes, so they pass through the small intestine and into the large bowel. This low digestibility helps explain the best-known effects of dietary fiber—promotion of regularity, relief from constipation and protection against diverticular disease and colorectal cancer. Constipation occurs when there is insufficient moist bulk for proper intestinal muscular contraction; this leads to straining, which can cause painful hernias in the colon wall (diverticuli). Fiber promotes bulk and water retention, so that muscular contraction is easier. Fiber-rich foods are excellent for relieving simple constipation.

Obviously, foods are the preferred source of fiber (especially whole grain products, legumes, fruits and vegetables), as they provide other nutrients. However, people with food intolerances can take supplements (for example, psyllium) that can help maintain adequate fiber intake.

Dietary fiber recommendations for people under 50 are 38 g for men and 25 g for women. For people over 50 years, the figures are 30 g for men and 25 g for women.

An adequate intake of dietary fiber becomes even more important when you are on a weight-loss diet. Our volunteers reported that their usual dietary fiber intake was insufficient to maintain regularity once they started dieting. It's important to adjust your food intake to ensure that you maintain normal function and comfort. Although the Total Wellbeing Diet ensures adequate fiber intake (30 g a day) through whole grain products, fruits and vegetables, you can increase your intake by consuming specific high-fiber foods if need be. A good high-bran cereal is a must if your bowels come to a halt when losing weight. Fiber-rich foods may be ineffective for people with irritable bowel syndrome, for whom products such as probiotics may be of assistance. Probiotics are foods containing live bacterial cultures, such as some yogurts.

There is evidence that a high-fiber diet reduces the risk of bowel cancer. People who eat diets rich in fiber typically have high stool weights with a rapid transit through the gut, which reduces the extent to which the gut is exposed to cancer-causing chemicals. Possibly more important, however, is the capacity of the bacteria in the large bowel to break these sugars down into gas, water and short-chain fatty acids that we can use as food. These short-chain fatty acids include butyric acid, which gut cells use as food and which can stop the growth of bowel cancer cells in a test tube and make them behave more like normal cells. The process may also release trapped minerals such as calcium and make the bowel contents more acidic. These two effects may make cancer-producing chemicals less active.

## Low-GI carbohydrates—keeping your blood glucose levels on an even keel

All carbohydrate foods have an effect on your blood glucose levels. But we now know that the rise-and-fall effect varies significantly depending on the kind of carbohydrate you eat. Think of the glycemic index (GI) simply as a way of measuring that effect. Research has shown that slowly digested or low-GI carbohydrates produce less fluctuation and thus help keep your blood glucose on an even keel. One reason why whole grain cereals contribute to improved health is that their starch is digested more slowly.

Foods with a high GI, on the other hand, produce a marked rise and fall in blood glucose levels after consumption. Highly refined processed foods tend to be digested rapidly by the stomach and small intestine. Starch is broken down to glucose, which is absorbed and enters the bloodstream. Blood glucose levels begin to climb within 30 minutes of eating a meal, triggering an increase in insulin secretion by the pancreas, which leads to a fall in glucose by uptake into body tissues. This rise in blood glucose following a meal is called the glycemic response and is most pronounced when pure glucose is ingested, since it is absorbed very quickly. The demand for insulin is also high following consumption of refined starch.

Chronically elevated blood glucose and plasma insulin are features of obesity and can lead to the development of type 2 diabetes. In the long term, raised blood glucose is a health risk, and there is good evidence that a modest loss of body weight can normalize blood glucose levels. Foods that provoke this raised blood glucose response are defined as having a high GI. Such foods should be avoided as much as possible and replaced with low-GI foods. Alternatively, high-GI foods should be eaten in smaller amounts.

### What is the GI?

The GI of a food is obtained by graphing someone's blood glucose after they have eaten an amount of a test food containing 50 g of available carbohydrate and comparing it to the blood glucose response to 50 g of pure glucose. GI is simply a value expressed as a percentage and foods are classified as low, medium or high GI. It is becoming very clear that many processed foods have a high GI, while some less processed foods (including some types of rice and potatoes) have a similar GI to glucose. Generally speaking, though, the less refined a food is, the lower the GI.

Foods with a low GI include legumes and many whole grain cereals. The intact dietary fiber and other components in these foods limit the access of enzymes to the starch, which means it takes longer to digest. Some foods, such as legumes, contain natural compounds that inhibit the action of the enzyme that breaks down starch. In some cases, the physical nature of the starch also has an effect. For example, a specific starch from corn resists digestion because of its composition, and corn therefore has a low GI.

## Glycemic load—combining carbohydrate quality and quantity

Talking about the GI of foods can be misleading, because, for example, although you need to eat about three slices of white bread to ingest 50 g of carbohydrate, one 1 oz slice of bread is a considered to be a serving. To solve this problem, the concept of glycemic load (GL) was developed. GL is the GI of the food multiplied by the amount of carbohydrate in a serving. The GL therefore takes into account both the type of carbohydrate and the amount. This means that eating a lot of a low-GI food (such as pasta) can result in a higher GL and eating a little of a high-GI food (such as carrots) can result in a low GL. People who eat low-GL foods have a lower risk of serious illness and obesity. The carbohydrate sources recommended in the Total Wellbeing Diet are generally low in GI, and because the total amount of carbohydrate in the Diet is controlled, the Diet is low in GL.

## Whole grains and resistant starch

The concept of resistant starch is a natural extension of GI and GL. The slower digestion of starch in low-GI foods in the small intestine means that, as a meal moves along, a significant fraction of starch escapes into the large intestine (bowel). This fraction is called resistant starch, as it resists digestion by the small intestine. Resistant starch occurs for a variety of reasons: for example, uncooked starches are hard for human enzymes to digest because the granules are tightly packed; and the dietary fiber in whole grain cereals restricts access of enzymes.

In some ways, resistant starch resembles dietary fiber. However, resistant starch differs in that all of its benefits are mediated through its metabolic products made by bacteria. The human colon is home to a population of bacteria that exceeds the number of cells in the human body. These bacteria are largely benign and digest resistant starch (and some fiber), obtaining energy in the process. This energy fuels further bacterial growth and yields short-chain fatty acids, which are useful for us. In fact, these simple acids seem to effect some of the actions we thought were due solely to fiber. Short-chain fatty acids are weak acids and so help to keep potentially harmful bacteria in check. They are taken up from the colon, provide energy for the lining cells and help maintain their integrity. Their uptake is accompanied by the absorption of water, sodium and potassium, which assists in the prevention and management of diarrhea. They may also help lower the risk of colon cancer, the third most common cancer in America.

## Choosing your breads and cereals

Whole grain breads and high-fiber cereals feature in the Diet recipes and menus. On a typical day on the Diet, you eat two 1 oz slices (2 units) of whole grain bread. You can replace one unit each day with any of the following:

- ⅓ cup baked beans, or cooked lentils, kidney beans or other beans (the best choice)
- 1 x 1 oz slice fruit loaf (another good choice)
- 2 crispbread, such as Ryvita
- 1 medium potato (about 5 oz)
- ⅓ cup cooked rice or noodles
- ½ cup cooked pasta.

You also eat one unit per day of high-fiber cereal. This is equal to:

- 1 Weetabix or Original Shredded Wheat plus ½ cup All-Bran
- 1½ oz any high-fiber breakfast cereal (e.g., Raisin Bran, Fiber One)
- 1 x 1 oz slice whole grain toast.

# Fats and oils

Fat is remarkable stuff. It keeps us warm, protects our internal organs, stores calories for a rainy day, forms the basis of cell membranes and also acts as a signaling molecule. It's also a very concentrated source of energy, with more than twice as many calories per ounce as protein or carbohydrate, so we only need a small amount each day—about the equivalent of 3 teaspoons.

We are often asked, "Does fat make you fat?" What makes you fat is eating more than your body burns. Eating too much of any food type (protein, fat, alcohol and carbohydrate) will result in weight gain. However, fat does have more calories per gram than the rest. But we rarely eat fat on its own. Any calorie-rich food that is easy to eat in large amounts—such as soft drinks, cakes, pastries, candy and cookies—will be unhelpful in controlling weight if eaten in excess, whether or not their fat content is high. Always check the total calories on food labels, not just the fat.

The Total Wellbeing Diet is low in fat. Less than 30 percent of your daily calories will be derived from fat on this diet compared with a typical American diet, where 34 percent comes from fat. That's why we specify lean red meats, skinless chicken and low-fat dairy products in the menus and recipes. Not only that, the fats we recommend you eat as spreads or use in your cooking or for making salad dressings are what we call the "good fats."

So what are the good fats? Fats can be divided into two broad classes: saturated (bad) and unsaturated (good). You can tell them apart. Saturated fats are solid at room temperature. These are the fats on meat or chicken skin, butter, cheese, palm oil and coconut oil. Eating lots of foods with these fats may raise your blood cholesterol. We don't actually need to eat any saturated fat, since the body can make all it requires, but it is fairly difficult not to eat some, since all fats are actually mixtures of saturated and unsaturated fats. In fact, saturated fats are really just high in saturated fat and low in unsaturated fat.

Unsaturated fat is liquid at room temperature. It's important in making our cell membranes fluid so they function correctly. Your body can make the most abundant unsaturated fat, oleic acid, very easily, but you can also get it from olive oil and canola oil, which are both monounsaturated. Polyunsaturated fats include linoleic acid (in safflower and sunflower oils), fish oils and oils from seeds, while monounsaturated fats are found in avocado and almonds and the oils derived from these foods.

## The essential fatty acids—omega-3 and omega-6

We looked at some of the good fats earlier with the omega-3 story and the benefits of eating fish (pages 41–42). There's more to it. We also need a minimum of 1–2 g a day of an omega-6 fatty acid called linoleic acid. This oil is essential and is involved in the proper functioning of skin cells—people with a deficiency suffer from rashes and poor skin function. Linoleic acid also lowers cholesterol, and there is evidence that taking in more of it, perhaps as much as 20 g a day, can help prevent heart disease. Good sources are safflower oil, sunflower oil, peanut oil, nuts and seeds.

## Trans fatty acids

Trans fatty acids are unsaturated fatty acids that behave like saturated fats, raising blood cholesterol and increasing the risk of heart disease. They are found at low levels in dairy foods and beef, and are present in margarines and baking fats.

As the Total Wellbeing Diet is low in fat, you will only be eating around 3 teaspoons of margarine (or 6 teaspoons of a light margarine) a day at the most, so your intake of trans fatty acids will be negligible.

## Cholesterol

Cholesterol is a type of fat, but it is not an energy source; the body produces all it needs to make cell membranes, sex hormones and bile acids. Dietary cholesterol can raise blood cholesterol in some people, but in most people the effect is minimal. Most often, high blood cholesterol is a result of a diet high in saturated fat. However, if your cholesterol is very high and you have heart disease or are at high risk of heart disease, it's best to limit foods high in cholesterol. The main sources of dietary cholesterol are eggs and organ meats, but it also occurs at low levels in all animal products, such as meat, milk,  cheese and butter. That's why on the Total Wellbeing Diet, our menus and recipes use lean meats, low-fat dairy foods and light margarine.

### *Plant sterols—reducing blood cholesterol*

Plant sterols are the plant equivalent of cholesterol, but they are good for you. Large amounts of plant sterols, or similar compounds called stanols, throw cholesterol out of the absorption packets that have arrived at the gut wall ready to be taken up into the body. As there is now less cholesterol in each packet, less cholesterol is absorbed, which in 80 percent of people leads to a drop in blood cholesterol. Gut cells can tell the difference between cholesterol and sterol, and absorb the sterol to only a limited extent (5 percent or less).

Diets including lots of plant foods are higher in sterols, but to get a measurable effect on blood cholesterol levels, sterols must be taken in higher quantities. In America, they have been added to some margarines and may soon become available in yogurt, milk and other foods. You need to eat about 4–5 teaspoons a day of sterol-enriched margarine to experience a 10 percent reduction in blood cholesterol. Eating more than this does not usually produce a greater effect. The low-fat versions of these enriched margarines are best for weight-control diets.

## Choosing your fats and oils

On the Total Wellbeing Diet we allow 3 teaspoons (3 units) of added fats/oils a day. This includes any liquid oil such as canola, olive or sunflower oil. 3 units oil is equal to:
- 3 teaspoons soft margarine (note 2 teaspoons light margarine = 1 teaspoon oil)
- 3 teaspoons curry paste in canola oil
- 2 oz avocado
- 1 oz nuts or seeds
- 3 teaspoons peanut butter

# alcohol

Alcohol is one of life's simple pleasures and in moderation can be an integral part of a healthy and balanced lifestyle if you want it to be. On the Total Wellbeing Diet you can enjoy 2 standard drinks a week if you wish. Two glasses of wine (10 oz) is equivalent to two standard drinks of any alcoholic beverage (see What's a standard drink? page 61). This is well within the recommended guidelines for safe intake.

Moderate drinking can promote health, but the harmful consequences of excessive alcohol intake are devastating. Alcohol also slows down fat metabolism—a big consideration when you need to lose weight and excess tummy fat.

It goes without saying that your body's ability to burn (metabolize) fat is vitally important for weight loss. If the burning of fat is prevented, the fat stores don't go away, but tend to accumulate. As we explained in Chapter 2, your daily calorie needs are supplied by what you eat or drink (the protein, carbohydrate and fat in food) and by your body's energy stores—essential when you need to lose that tummy fat. It is useful to understand that your body breaks down food and drink in a certain order. As your body has nowhere to store unused alcohol, it uses alcohol first to produce calories. Pro-tein comes second, followed by carbohydrate, and finally fat. So alcohol prevents fat from being used by the body.

There are a couple of other good reasons why it's important to keep your consumption of alcohol right down when you need to lose weight. First of all, alcohol is a significant source of calories. One gram of alcohol provides 7 calories. This adds up to a grand total of 100 calories in a standard 5 oz glass of wine, 150 calories in a 12 oz can of beer and even more in mixed drinks with added fruit juice or soft drinks—and all without satisfying your appetite at all, nor adding any essential micronutrients to your diet. (See the table on page 61 for the calorie count of some popular drinks.) In addition, because alcohol stimulates the biochemical pathways involved in appetite control, it's all too easy to end up overeating. We are not saying that you need to become a teetotaler to lose weight, but limiting your alcohol consumption will have positive benefits for weight loss and maintenance. For weight maintenance and on special occasions, 2 standard drinks for women and 4 standard drinks for men is a safe amount to drink.

## health benefits of moderate alcohol consumption

Moderate drinking has been shown to have some positive health benefits—so there's no need to throw the baby out with the bathwater and become a teetotaler! Drinking one to two standard drinks per day may actually afford a health benefit for many people.

An alcohol intake of two standard drinks per day has been associated with reduced risk of coronary heart disease. This seems to be because alcohol increases the level of HDL cholesterol ("good" cholesterol), which helps remove cholesterol from the artery to the liver for excretion. It also seems to reduce the formation of blood clots.

Some studies have shown that moderate wine drinkers have better protection against death from coronary heart disease than moderate beer and spirit drinkers. But this could be because those who prefer wine may smoke less and have a healthier diet high in fruits and vegetables, olive oil and fish. However, the added protection could be due in part to some other component in wine, such as the phenolic compounds, which have antioxidant properties (see page 48).

Alcohol also has a beneficial effect on insulin sensitivity, promoting a more efficient use of glucose by the body and reducing the risk of type 2 diabetes. Moderate alcohol consumption seems to protect against dementia as well. It is likely that the benefits of alcohol intake in protection against vascular and neurological disease depend largely on an individual's genes.

The jury is still out as to whether low to moderate alcohol consumption provides any real protection against cancer risk. Some studies have shown that where alcohol intake is more than 5 oz a day (about one glass of wine) the risk of cancer is increased. The best evidence for this is in breast cancer studies. CSIRO studies have shown that while the alcohol in wines clearly damages DNA and sensitizes cells to harmful free radicals, the plant polyphenols catechin and gallic acid (the nonalcoholic components of wines) protect the DNA from damage by free radicals.

## What's a standard drink?

In the U.S., a standard drink contains about 14 grams or 0.6 fluid ounces of pure alcohol. Different alcoholic beverages vary widely in the amount of alcohol they contain. The table below will be helpful, but you need to check each label carefully.

**STANDARD DRINKS AND CALORIE COUNTS OF ALCOHOLIC BEVERAGES**

| drink | type | amount | calories |
|---|---|---|---|
| wine | white, dry | 5 oz | 100 |
| | white, sweet | 5 oz | 110 |
| | white, sparkling | 5 oz | 110 |
| | red | 5 oz | 100 |
| | red, sparkling | 5 oz | 110 |
| beer | regular | 12 oz | 150 |
| | lite | 12 oz | 110 |
| | nonalcohol | 12 oz | 150 |
| | stout | 12 oz | 155 |
| liquor* | nonsweet | 1.5 oz | 100 |
| liqueur* | cream-based | 1.5 oz | 160 |

*These calories are for the alcohol only. If you are drinking a mixed drink, the number of calories will be increased by the mixers used. Some mixed drinks combine liquors and a single mixed drink can include the amount of liquor in two or more standard drinks.

# part two

## menu plans for the Total Wellbeing Diet

# week one

The following pages contain your 12 week menu plans. These menus are based on Level 1 of the diet and have been carefully calculated to include the recommended daily intake for each food group at this level, taking into account the ingredients within the recipes—for example, each day includes 2½ cups salad or cooked vegetables. (See pages 22–23 for more detail on Level 1, and for quantities of foods required at Levels 2–4 see table on page 30.)

Having said this, the menu plans are a guide only and you are welcome to substitute your favorite foods for those in the menu plans—as long as they are from the same food group and in the same quantity, for example, 1 cup salad instead of 1 cup steamed greens. The menus can really be as flexible as you are creative.

| | breakfast | lunch | dinner |
|---|---|---|---|
| day 1 | 1½ oz high-fiber breakfast cereal (e.g., Fiber One) with 8 oz low-fat milk & 1 sliced banana | Salmon & salad sandwich (2 slices whole grain bread with 3.5 oz canned salmon & ½ cup salad leaves)<br>1 low-fat cafe latte or low-fat cappuccino | 7 oz beef: Beef Provencal Casserole (see p 156)<br>1 cup steamed green beans<br>5 oz drained canned fruit with 8 oz low-fat dairy dessert (e.g., custard) |
| day 2 | 1 Weetabix or Original Shredded Wheat & ½ cup All-Bran with 8 oz low-fat milk & 2 tbsp raisins | Red Pepper & Tomato Soup (see p 92)<br>Ham & tomato toasted sandwich (2 slices whole grain bread with 3.5 oz ham & slices of tomato)<br>1 piece fresh fruit | 7 oz chicken: Chicken Stir-fry with Broccoli & Red Pepper (see p 141)<br>½ cup steamed bok choy<br>8 oz low-fat yogurt |
| day 3 | 2 slices whole grain toast with 2 tsp light margarine<br>8 oz low-fat yogurt | 3.5 oz skinless cooked chicken<br>1½ cups salad with oil-free salad dressing<br>2 crispbreads (e.g., Ryvita)<br>1 piece fresh fruit | 7 oz fish: Barbecued Swordfish with Vegetables & Olives (see p 132)<br>Fruit Salad (see p 182) with 8 oz low-fat dairy dessert (e.g., custard) |
| day 4 | 1½ oz high-fiber breakfast cereal (e.g., Raisin Bran) with 8 oz low-fat milk & 5 oz drained canned fruit | Salmon roll (1 whole grain bread roll [2.5 oz] with 3.5 oz canned salmon & chopped onion)<br>Greek Salad (see p 101) | 7 oz lamb: Baked Rack of Lamb with Baby Vegetables (see p 169)<br>1 piece fresh fruit |
| day 5 | 1½ oz oatmeal with 8 oz low-fat milk & 3.5 oz low-fat yogurt | Corned beef & salad sandwich (2 slices whole grain bread with 3.5 oz corned beef, pickles & ½ cup salad leaves)<br>½ cup salad with oil-free salad dressing<br>1 piece fresh fruit | 7 oz fish: Char-grilled Salmon with Parsley Relish, Squash & Asparagus (see p 128)<br>1 piece fresh fruit<br>8 oz low-fat yogurt |
| day 6 | 2 slices whole grain raisin toast with 2 tsp light margarine<br>1 piece fresh fruit<br>1 low-fat cafe latte or low-fat cappuccino | Chicken & salad sandwich (2 slices whole grain bread with 3.5 oz cooked chicken, 1.5 oz avocado & ½ cup salad leaves)<br>½ cup salad with oil-free salad dressing<br>8 oz low-fat dairy dessert (e.g., custard) | 7 oz beef: Char-grilled Beef Filet with Mushrooms & Caramelized Onion (see p 157)<br>1 piece fresh fruit |
| day 7 | Scrambled Eggs (see p 112), with tomato, mushrooms & 2 pieces lean bacon, pan-fried in 1 tsp oil<br>2 slices whole grain toast with 2 tsp light margarine<br>1 low-fat cafe latte or low-fat cappuccino<br>1 small glass orange juice | brunch | 7 oz lamb: Lamb Kebabs (see p 166)<br>2 cups salad<br>⅓ cup cooked rice<br>Baked Pineapple (see p 184) with 8 oz low-fat yogurt |

• see pages 203–7 for weekly shopping lists
  note: if on 3 dairy servings (see page 22), use 1½ oz protein plus 1 extra dairy option

week two

| | breakfast | lunch | dinner |
|---|---|---|---|
| **day 1** | 1 piece fresh fruit<br>8 oz low-fat yogurt | Ham & cheese sandwich (2 slices whole grain bread with 2 tsp light margarine, 3.5 oz ham & 2.5 oz low-fat cheese)<br>1½ cups salad with oil-free salad dressing | 7 oz beef: Beef, Shiitake Mushroom & Snow Pea Stir-fry (see p 152)<br>⅓ cup cooked rice<br>1 piece fresh fruit |
| **day 2** | 1½ oz high-fiber breakfast cereal (e.g., Fiber One) with 8 oz low-fat milk & 1 sliced banana | Turkey & salad sandwich (2 slices whole grain bread with 3.5 oz turkey, cranberry sauce & ½ cup salad leaves)<br>2.5 oz low-fat cheese | 7 oz chicken: Chicken, Tomato & Rosemary Hotpot (see p 146)<br>1 cup salad with oil-free salad dressing<br>5 oz drained canned fruit |
| **day 3** | 2 slices whole grain toast with 2 tsp light margarine & 2 oz low-fat cheese | Egg & salad sandwich (2 slices whole grain bread with 2 hard-boiled eggs, slices of spring onions & ½ cup salad leaves)<br>1 piece fresh fruit | Light Vegetable Soup (see p 94)<br>8 oz fish: Cajun Fish Filets (see p 131)<br>1 cup steamed broccoli & carrot<br>5 oz drained canned fruit |
| **day 4** | 1 Weetabix or Original Shredded Wheat & ½ cup All-Bran with 8 oz low-fat milk & 1 sliced banana | Tuna with Cannellini Bean & Basil Salad (see p 101) | 7 oz beef: Roast Beef with Beet, Squash & Carrot (see p 158)<br>1 cup steamed zucchini & snow peas<br>1 piece fresh fruit<br>8 oz low-fat yogurt |
| **day 5** | 2 servings French Toast (see p 116)<br>1 small glass orange juice | Beef & Vegetable Soup (see p 94)<br>1 slice whole grain bread<br>2.5 oz low-fat cheese | 7 oz fish: Baked Snapper with Basil, Capers & Tomato (see p 134)<br>1 cup salad with oil-free salad dressing<br>Stewed Rhubarb (see p 184) with 8 oz low-fat dairy dessert (e.g., custard) |
| **day 6** | 1½ oz high-fiber breakfast cereal (e.g., Fiber One) with 4 oz low-fat milk and 8 oz low-fat yogurt<br>1 piece fresh fruit | Butternut Squash & Cilantro Soup (see p 92) with 2 oz cooked, chopped bacon added<br>1 slice whole grain bread with 2 oz ham & ½ cup salad leaves | 7 oz lamb: Indian Lamb & Spinach Curry (see p 166)<br>⅓ cup cooked rice<br>5 oz drained canned fruit |
| **day 7** | 1 egg (poached, boiled or scrambled), with ½ tomato & mushrooms pan-fried in 1 tsp oil<br>1 slice whole grain toast | Smoked salmon sandwich (2 slices whole grain bread with 2 oz low-fat cream cheese & 1 oz smoked salmon)<br>1 cup salad with oil-free salad dressing<br>1 piece fresh fruit | 7 oz veal: Seeded-mustard Rack of Veal with Roasted Vegetables (see p 159)<br>5 oz drained canned fruit with 8 oz low-fat dairy dessert (e.g., ice cream) |

• see pages 203–7 for weekly shopping lists
  note: if on 3 dairy servings (see page 22), use 1½ oz protein plus 1 extra dairy option

week three

| | breakfast | lunch | dinner |
|---|---|---|---|
| day 1 | 2 slices whole grain toast with 2 tsp light margarine & 2 oz low-fat cheese<br>1 low-fat cafe latte or low-fat cappuccino | Light Vegetable Soup (see p 94)<br>Open roast beef sandwich (1 slice whole grain bread with 1 tsp light margarine, 3.5 oz cold roast beef & ½ cup salad leaves)<br>1 piece fresh fruit | 7 oz fish: Swordfish Steaks with Warm Zucchini & Olive Salad (see p 128)<br>Stewed Rhubarb (see p 184) with 8 oz low-fat dairy dessert (e.g., custard) |
| day 2 | 1½ oz high-fiber breakfast cereal (e.g., Raisin Bran) with 8 oz low-fat milk & 1 sliced banana | Baked Potato with Ham, Rosemary & Cheddar (see p 116) | 7 oz beef: Meatballs in Tomato & Basil Sauce (see p 154)<br>1½ cups salad with oil-free salad dressing<br>1 piece fresh fruit |
| day 3 | 1 Weetabix or Original Shredded Wheat & ½ cup All-Bran with 4 oz low-fat milk & 1 sliced banana<br>1 slice raisin whole grain toast with 1 tsp light margarine | Salmon Salad with Tarragon & Caper Dressing (see p 102)<br>1 slice whole grain bread<br>1 piece fresh fruit | Light Vegetable Soup (see p 94)<br>7 oz chicken: Chicken with Dijon Mustard & White Wine (see p 142)<br>1 cup steamed green beans<br>8 oz low-fat yogurt |
| day 4 | 1½ oz instant oatmeal cooked with 8 oz low-fat milk<br>5 oz drained canned fruit | Ham & salad sandwich (2 slices whole grain bread with 3.5 oz ham, 1 oz avocado & ½ cup salad leaves) | 7 oz lamb: Italian Lamb Casserole (see p 167)<br>1 cup steamed broccoli & cauliflower<br>Stewed apple (see p 184) with 8 oz low-fat dairy dessert (e.g., custard) |
| day 5 | 1½ oz high-fiber breakfast cereal (e.g., All-Bran) with 8 oz low-fat milk | 4 crispbreads (e.g., Ryvita) with 3.5 oz canned tuna, 1 cup arugula leaves & 1 oz cheese<br>1 piece fresh fruit<br>8 oz low-fat yogurt | 7 oz veal: cutlets sprayed with olive oil & grilled or barbecued (see p 201), & topped with Pesto (see p 122)<br>1 cup (4 spears) steamed asparagus<br>Stewed apple (see p 184) |
| day 6 | 2 slices whole grain raisin toast with 2 tsp light margarine<br>Fruit smoothie (see p 182) | Beautiful Borscht (see p 94)<br>1 slice whole grain bread with 3.5 oz lean ham<br>1 piece fresh fruit | 2-egg Omelette (see p 112)<br>1½ cups salad with oil-free salad dressing<br>8 oz low-fat dairy dessert (e.g., ice cream) |
| day 7 | 1 egg (poached or boiled), with ½ tomato & mushrooms pan-fried in 1 tsp oil<br>1 slice whole grain toast with 1 tsp light margarine<br>1 small glass orange juice | Chicken & salad sandwich (2 slices whole grain bread with 2 oz cooked chicken, chutney & ½ cup salad leaves)<br>1 piece fresh fruit<br>8 oz low-fat yogurt | 7 oz lamb: Spiced Lamb Chops with Ratatouille (see p 163)<br>8 oz low-fat dairy dessert (e.g., frozen yogurt) |

• see pages 203–7 for weekly shopping lists
note: if on 3 dairy servings (see page 22), use 1½ oz protein plus 1 extra dairy option

week four

| | breakfast | lunch | dinner |
|---|---|---|---|
| day 1 | 2 slices whole grain raisin toast with 2 tsp light margarine<br>1 low-fat cafe latte or low-fat cappuccino | Roast Beef & Beet Salad (see p 107)<br>2 crispbreads (e.g., Ryvita)<br>1 piece fresh fruit | 7 oz beef: Char-grilled Beef Filet with Mushrooms & Caramelized Onion (see p 157)<br>Poached Pears with Blue Cheese (see p 182) |
| day 2 | 1½ oz high-fiber breakfast cereal (e.g., Fiber One) with 8 oz low-fat milk<br>1 piece fresh fruit | Pastrami & salad sandwich (2 slices whole grain bread with 2 tsp light margarine, 3.5 oz pastrami, slices of cucumber & tomato)<br>1 piece fresh fruit | 7 oz chicken: Baked Yogurt Chicken with Tomato, Mint & Cucumber Salad (see p 145)<br>1 cup baked cubes squash<br>8 oz low-fat yogurt |
| day 3 | 1½ oz instant oatmeal cooked with 8 oz low-fat milk, with 2 tbsp raisins or dried apple | Butternut Squash & Cilantro Soup (see p 92)<br>Ham & salad roll (1 whole grain bread roll [2.5 oz] with 3.5 oz ham, mustard, slices of tomato & ½ cup salad leaves) | 7 oz fish: Moroccan Snapper Filets (see p 134)<br>1 cup steamed green beans and carrot<br>1 piece fresh fruit<br>8 oz low-fat yogurt |
| day 4 | Fresh Fruit Salad (see p 182) with 8 oz low-fat yogurt<br>1 slice whole grain toast with 1 tsp light margarine | 4 crispbreads (e.g., Ryvita) with 2 tsp light cream cheese, 3.5 oz smoked salmon, capers & ½ cup salad leaves<br>1 low-fat cafe latte or low-fat cappuccino | 7 oz lamb: Rosemary & Lemon Lamb Cutlets with Baked Fennel & Red Onion (see p 162)<br>1 cup salad with oil-free salad dressing<br>1 piece fresh fruit |
| day 5 | 2 servings Fresh Fruit Salad (see page 182) with 8 oz low-fat yogurt | Burger (see p 156)<br>½ cup salad with oil-free salad dressing | 7 oz fish: Seafood Paella (see p 136)<br>1 cup steamed green beans & broccoli<br>1 piece fresh fruit with 8 oz low-fat dairy dessert (e.g., custard) |
| day 6 | Grilled cheese & tomato on toast (2 slices whole grain bread with 1 oz cheddar cheese, slices of tomato & cracked pepper)<br>1 piece fresh fruit | 1 lunch serving Thai Beef Salad (see p 108)<br>8 oz low-fat yogurt | 7 oz lamb: Spiced Lamb Filets with Broccolini (see p 164)<br>⅓ cup cooked rice<br>Fresh Fruit Salad (see p 182) |
| day 7 | Scrambled Eggs (see p 112), with tomato & mushrooms pan-fried in 1 tsp oil<br>1 slice whole grain toast with 1 tsp light margarine | Cheese & salad roll (1 whole grain bread roll [2.5 oz] with 2 oz low-fat cheese, mustard, slices of tomato, beets & red onion, & ½ cup salad leaves)<br>1 piece fresh fruit | 7 oz beef: Roast Beef with Beets, Squash & Carrot (see p 158)<br>1 piece fresh fruit<br>8 oz low-fat dairy dessert (e.g., frozen yogurt) |

• see pages 203–7 for weekly shopping lists
note: if on 3 dairy servings (see page 22), use 1½ oz protein plus 1 extra dairy option

week five

| | breakfast | lunch | dinner |
|---|---|---|---|
| day 1 | 1½ oz high-fiber breakfast cereal with 8 oz low-fat milk<br>1 piece fresh fruit | Roast beef wrap (1 whole grain Lebanese flatbread with 2 tsp light margarine, 3.5 oz rare roast beef, horseradish, slices of cucumber & tomato & ½ cup arugula leaves) | 7 oz beef: Meatballs in Tomato & Basil Sauce (see p 154)<br>½ cup steamed green beans<br>5 oz drained canned fruit with 8 oz low-fat dairy dessert |
| day 2 | 1 whole grain English muffin with 1 tsp light margarine & low-calorie jam<br>1 low-fat cafe latte or low-fat cappuccino<br>1 piece fresh fruit | Pastrami sandwich (2 slices whole grain bread with 2 tsp light margarine, 3.5 oz pastrami, 2 oz low-fat cheddar cheese, slices of onion & ½ cup salad leaves) | 7 oz fish: White fish filets in Seafood marinade (see p 124), grilled or barbecued (see p 201)<br>2 cups salad with oil-free salad dressing<br>1 piece fresh fruit |
| day 3 | 1½ oz instant oatmeal cooked with 8 oz low-fat milk<br>1 piece fresh fruit | 1 slice whole grain toast with ½ cup baked beans<br>1½ cups salad with 2 oz avocado & oil-free salad dressing<br>1 piece fresh fruit | 7 oz lamb: Cilantro & Chili Pepper Lamb Kebabs (see p 166)<br>1 cup steamed broccoli & carrots<br>8 oz low-fat yogurt |
| day 4 | 1½ oz high-fiber breakfast cereal with 4 oz low-fat milk & 8 oz low-fat yogurt<br>1 piece fresh fruit | Roast Red Pepper & Tomato Soup (see p 92)<br>Salmon & salad roll (1 whole grain bread roll [2.5 oz] with 3.5 oz canned salmon, chopped onion & ½ cup salad leaves) | 7 oz chicken: Stir-fried Ginger Chicken with Sesame Bok Choy (see p 140)<br>1 piece fresh fruit |
| day 5 | 1½ oz high-fiber breakfast cereal with 8 oz low-fat milk<br>1 piece fresh fruit | Turkey roll (1 whole grain bread roll [2.5 oz] with 2 tsp light margarine, 3.5 oz turkey & cranberry sauce)<br>Greek Salad (see p 101) | 7 oz fish: White fish filets in Chili & Lime marinade (see p 123), grilled or barbecued (see p 201)<br>1½ cups salad with oil-free salad dressing<br>1 piece fresh fruit |
| day 6 | 2 slices whole grain raisin toast with 2 tsp light margarine<br>1 low-fat cafe latte or low-fat cappuccino | 1 slice whole grain toast with 3.5 oz sardines & slices of tomato<br>1½ cups salad with oil-free salad dressing<br>1 piece fresh fruit | 7 oz lamb: 1 dinner serving Warm Salad of Moroccan Lamb with Roasted Tomatoes (see p 108)<br>Fresh Fruit Salad (see p 182) with 8 oz low-fat yogurt |
| day 7 | 1 egg (poached, boiled or scrambled), with ½ tomato pan-fried in 1 tsp light margarine<br>1 slice whole grain toast with 1 tsp light margarine | Tuna & salad sandwich (2 slices whole grain bread with 2 oz canned tuna, 2 oz low-fat ricotta, slices of cucumber & ½ cup salad leaves)<br>1 piece fresh fruit | 7 oz beef: Beef Provençal Casserole (see p 156)<br>1 cup steamed green beans and carrot<br>Stewed Rhubarb (see p 184) with 8 oz low-fat dairy dessert |

• see pages 203–7 for weekly shopping lists
note: if on 3 dairy servings (see page 22), use 1½ oz protein plus 1 extra dairy option

week six

| | breakfast | lunch | dinner |
|---|---|---|---|
| day 1 | 1½ oz high-fiber breakfast cereal with 8 oz low-fat milk<br>1 piece fresh fruit | Roast beef sandwich (2 slices rye bread with 3.5 oz rare roast beef, horseradish, slices of pepper & ½ cup salad leaves)<br>1 piece fresh fruit | 7 oz fish: pan-fried white fish filets (see p 201) & top with Olive Tapenade (see p 120)<br>2 cups steamed carrots & broccoli<br>8 oz low-fat dairy dessert |
| day 2 | 1 slice whole grain toast with 1 tsp light margarine<br>Stewed fruit (see p 184) with 8 oz low-fat yogurt | Ham & cheese toasted sandwich (2 slices whole grain bread with 3.5 oz ham, 2 oz low-fat cheese & slices of tomato & pickles)<br>½ cup salad with oil-free salad dressing | 7 oz beef: Beef & Potato Pie (see p 154)<br>½ cup boiled peas<br>1 piece fresh fruit |
| day 3 | 1½ oz high-fiber breakfast cereal with 8 oz low-fat milk & 2 tbsp dried fruit | Salmon salad (3.5 oz canned salmon, 1½ cups chopped salad vegetables, 1 oz low-fat cheese, 2 oz avocado & 1 tbsp oil-free mayonnaise)<br>4 whole grain crispbreads | 7 oz chicken: Tandoori Chicken with Garlic Spinach (see p 142)<br>1 piece fresh fruit |
| day 4 | 1 slice whole grain toast with ½ cup baked beans<br>1 piece fresh fruit | Light Vegetable Soup (see p 94)<br>Chicken, salad & pesto roll (1 small whole grain bread roll [2.5 oz] with 3.5 oz cooked chicken, 2 tsp pesto, 2 oz low-fat cheese & ½ cup salad leaves) | 7 oz lamb: Greek-style Lamb Kebabs with Tzatziki (see p 164)<br>1 cup spinach, steamed<br>Fresh Fruit Salad (see p 182) with 8 oz low-fat dairy dessert |
| day 5 | 1½ oz high-fiber breakfast cereal with 8 oz low-fat milk<br>1 piece fresh fruit | Open Steak Sandwich (see p 152) without avocado<br>½ cup salad with oil-free salad dressing<br>1 piece fresh fruit | 7 oz fish: grilled or barbecued salmon steaks (see p 201), topped with Miso Sesame Sauce (see p 121)<br>1½ cups steamed broccoli & bok choy<br>8 oz low-fat yogurt |
| day 6 | Banana Smoothie (see p 182)<br>1 piece focaccia bread with 1 tsp light margarine & low-calorie jam | 2 boiled eggs<br>1 cup salad with oil-free salad dressing<br>2 slices whole grain toast with 1 tsp light margarine | 7 oz beef: Thai Beef Salad (see p 108)<br>Stewed fruit (see p 184) with Baked Custard (see p 184) |
| day 7 | Scrambled Eggs (see p 112), with tomato, mushrooms & 2 oz spinach pan-fried in 1 tsp oil<br>1 slice rye toast with 1 tsp light margarine | Cheese & salad bagel (1 whole grain bagel with 2 oz low-fat ricotta, slices of cucumber & ½ cup salad leaves)<br>1 piece fresh fruit<br>4 oz low-fat yogurt | 7 oz lamb: Roast Leg of Lamb with Rosemary & Garlic (see p 171)<br>1½ cups steamed green beans & carrots<br>1 piece fresh fruit<br>4 oz low-fat ice cream |

• see pages 203–7 for weekly shopping lists
note: if on 3 dairy servings (see page 22), use 1½ oz protein plus 1 extra dairy option

week seven

| | breakfast | lunch | dinner |
|---|---|---|---|
| **day 1** | 1½ oz high-fiber breakfast cereal with 8 oz low-fat milk<br>1 piece fresh fruit | Salmon salad (3.5 oz canned salmon with 1½ cups tabouli made with oil-free salad dressing)<br>2 crispbreads with 2 tsp light margarine<br>8 oz low-fat yogurt | 7 oz beef: Veal Rolls in Tomato & Red Wine Sauce (see p 158)<br>1 boiled potato<br>Fresh Fruit salad (see p 182) |
| **day 2** | 1½ oz muesli (not toasted) with 8 oz low-fat yogurt & 5 oz drained canned fruit | Burger (see p 156)<br>½ cup salad with oil-free salad dressing<br>1 piece fresh fruit | 7 oz fish: marinate tuna steaks in Ginger Soy (see p 123) & pan-fry (see p 201)<br>1½ cups broccoli & snow peas & 1 tbsp flaked almonds, stir-fried in 1 tsp oil<br>8 oz low-fat dairy dessert |
| **day 3** | 1½ oz high-fiber breakfast cereal with 8 oz low-fat milk<br>1 piece fresh fruit | Pastrami wrap (1 whole grain Lebanese flatbread with 3.5 oz pastrami, pickles, slices of tomato & ½ cup baby spinach leaves) | 7 oz lamb: coat lamb steaks with Lamb Rub (see p 125) & grill or barbecue (see p 201)<br>Baked Mediterranean Vegetables with Ricotta (see p 179)<br>1 piece fresh fruit |
| **day 4** | Grilled cheese on toasted muffin (1 multigrain English muffin with 1 oz cheddar cheese & slices of tomato)<br>1 piece fresh fruit | Open ham & salad sandwich (1 slice whole grain bread with 3.5 oz ham, mustard, 2 oz avocado, slices of tomato & ½ cup salad leaves) | 7 oz chicken: Stir-fried Ginger Chicken with Sesame Bok Choy (see p 140)<br>1 cup steamed broccoli & carrot<br>Fresh Fruit Salad (see p 182) with 8 oz low-fat yogurt |
| **day 5** | 1 slice whole grain toast with 2 oz sardines & lemon juice<br>1 piece fresh fruit | Light Vegetable Soup (see p 94) with 2 oz chopped ham added<br>2 crispbreads with 1 tsp light margarine<br>8 oz low-fat yogurt | 7 oz fish: Seafood Paella (see p 136)<br>1 cup steamed green beans<br>1 piece fresh fruit<br>8 oz low-fat milk with cocoa & Equal |
| **day 6** | 2 whole grain English muffins with 2 tsp light margarine & low-calorie jam<br>1 piece fresh fruit<br>1 low-fat cafe latte or low-fat cappuccino | 1 lunch serving Warm Chicken Salad (see p 104) without avocado<br>8 oz low-fat yogurt | 7 oz beef: sprinkle rump steaks with lemon pepper & grill or barbecue (see p 201)<br>1½ cups steamed zucchini & carrot<br>1 boiled potato<br>1 piece fresh fruit |
| **day 7** | Egg & bacon sandwich (2 slices whole grain bread with 1 poached egg, 2 oz grilled lean bacon & ½ cup arugula)<br>1 low-fat cafe latte or low-fat cappuccino | Butternut Squash & Cilantro Soup (see p 92)<br>2 crispbreads with 2 tsp light margarine<br>5 oz drained canned fruit with 8 oz low-fat yogurt | 7 oz lamb: marinated diced lamb filet in Greek-style marinade (see p 124), threaded onto skewers, then barbecued (see p 201)<br>1 cup salad with oil-free salad dressing<br>1 piece fresh fruit |

• see pages 203–7 for weekly shopping lists
note: if on 3 dairy servings (see page 22), use 1½ oz protein plus 1 extra dairy option

# week eight

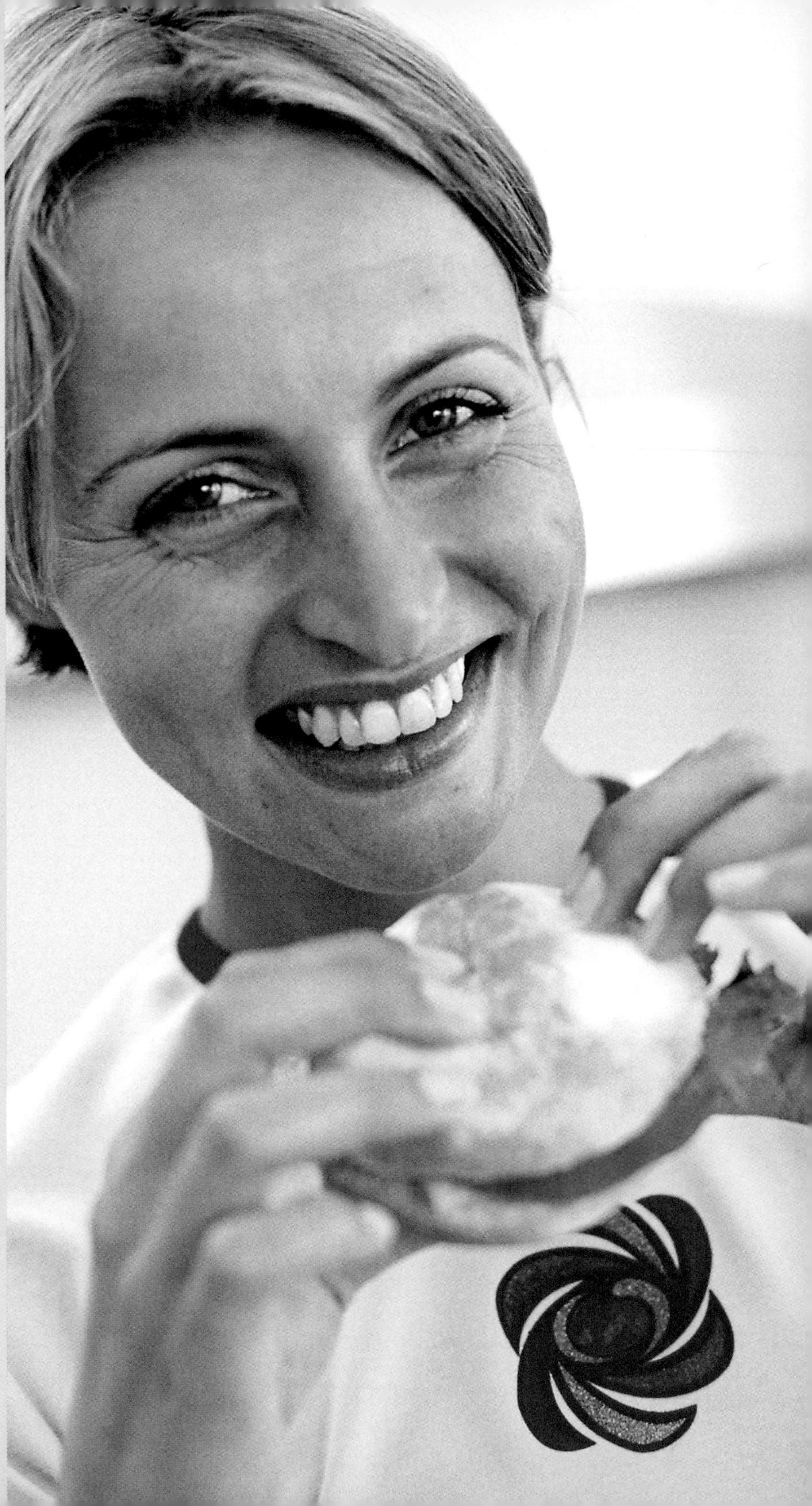

| | breakfast | lunch | dinner |
|---|---|---|---|
| **day 1** | 1½ oz instant oatmeal with 4 oz low-fat milk<br>Stewed apple (see p 184) | Chicken & salad sandwich (2 slices whole grain bread with 2 tsp light margarine, 3.5 oz skinless cooked chicken, chutney & ½ cup salad leaves)<br>1 piece fresh fruit | 7 oz beef: Meatballs in Tomato & Basil Sauce (see p 154)<br>1 cup steamed broccoli, carrots & beans<br>8 oz low-fat milk with cocoa & Equal |
| **day 2** | 1 slice whole grain raisin toast with 1 tsp light margarine<br>1 piece fresh fruit<br>1 low-fat cafe latte or low-fat cappuccino | Tuna & salad rollup (1 small whole grain pita bread with 3.5 oz canned tuna, slices of onion & peppers, ½ cup salad leaves & oil-free salad dressing)<br>1 piece fresh fruit | 7 oz chicken: Chicken, Tomato & Rosemary Hotpot (see p 146)<br>1 cup steamed green beans<br>8 oz low-fat dairy dessert |
| **day 3** | 1½ oz high-fiber breakfast cereal with 8 oz low-fat milk & 1 sliced banana<br>4 oz low-fat yogurt | 2 slices whole grain bread with 2 hard-boiled eggs<br>1 cup salad with oil-free salad dressing<br>1 low-fat cafe latte or low-fat cappuccino | 7 oz fish: Char-grilled Salmon with Parsley Relish, Squash, Asparagus (see p 128)<br>5 oz drained canned fruit |
| **day 4** | 2 whole grain English muffins with ⅓ cup baked beans<br>1 piece fresh fruit | Open ham & salad sandwich (1 slice whole grain bread with 3.5 oz ham, mustard, 1 oz cheese & ½ cup salad leaves)<br>1 piece fresh fruit | Light Vegetable Soup (see p 94)<br>7 oz lamb: Spiced Lamb Filets with Broccolini (see p 164)<br>8 oz low-fat yogurt |
| **day 5** | 1½ oz instant oatmeal cooked with 8 oz low-fat milk<br>1 slice whole grain toast with 1 tsp light margarine | Open corned beef & salad sandwich (1 slice whole grain bread with 3.5 oz corned beef, chutney, grated carrot & ½ cup salad leaves)<br>Banana Smoothie (see p 182) | 7 oz fish: grill or barbecue white fish filets (see p 201) & top with 1 tbsp Parsley Relish (see p 120)<br>2 cups steamed broccoli & cauliflower<br>Stewed Rhubarb (see p 184) |
| **day 6** | 1 Weetabix or Original Shredded Wheat & ½ cup All-Bran with 8 oz low-fat milk<br>5 oz canned fruit in natural juice | 1 slice whole grain bread with 3.5 oz canned salmon & 2 oz avocado<br>1½ cups salad with oil-free salad dressing | 7 oz beef: Beef, Shiitake Mushroom & Snow Pea Stir-fry (see p 152)<br>⅓ cup cooked rice<br>Fresh Fruit Salad (see p 182) with 8 oz low-fat yogurt |
| **day 7** | Fresh Fruit Salad (see p 182)<br>2 eggs (poached, boiled or scrambled), with ½ tomato & mushrooms pan-fried in 1 tsp oil<br>2 slices whole grain toast with 1 tsp light margarine<br>1 small glass orange juice<br>1 low-fat cafe latte or low-fat cappuccino | | Butternut Squash & Cilantro Soup (see p 92)<br>7 oz lamb: Baked Rack of Lamb with Baby Vegetables (see p 169)<br>8 oz low-fat dairy dessert |

• see pages 203–7 for weekly shopping lists
note: if on 3 dairy servings (see page 22), use 1½ oz protein plus 1 extra dairy option

week nine

| | breakfast | lunch | dinner |
|---|---|---|---|
| day 1 | 1½ oz high-fiber breakfast cereal with 8 oz low-fat milk<br>1 piece fresh fruit | Smoked salmon & salad wrap (1 whole grain Lebanese flatbread with 3.5 oz smoked salmon, alfalfa sprouts, slices of tomato, 2 oz avocado & ½ cup arugula leaves) | 7 oz beef: Veal Rolls in Tomato & Red Wine Sauce (see p 158)<br>1 cup steamed zucchini & carrots<br>5 oz drained canned fruit with 8 oz low-fat dairy dessert |
| day 2 | 1 whole grain English muffin with 1 tsp light margarine & low-calorie jam<br>1 piece fresh fruit<br>1 low-fat cafe latte or low-fat cappuccino | Pastrami & salad sandwich (2 slices whole grain bread with 2 oz pastrami, 1 oz low-fat cheddar cheese, slices of red onion & ½ cup salad leaves) | 7 oz fish: Baked Snapper with Basil, Capers & Tomato (see p 134)<br>1½ cups salad with oil-free salad dressing<br>Fresh Fruit Salad (see p 182) with 8 oz low-fat yogurt |
| day 3 | 1½ oz high-fiber breakfast cereal with 8 oz low-fat milk<br>1 piece fresh fruit | 1 slice whole grain toast with ½ cup baked beans<br>Ham salad (3.5 oz ham & 1 cup salad leaves tossed with balsamic vinegar & 1 tsp olive oil) | 7 oz lamb: Spiced Lamb Chops with Ratatouille (see p 163)<br>1 piece fresh fruit<br>8 oz low-fat yogurt |
| day 4 | 1½ oz high-fiber breakfast cereal with 8 oz low-fat milk<br>1 piece fresh fruit | Salmon & salad roll (1 whole grain bread roll [2.5 oz] with 3.5 oz canned salmon, chopped onion & ½ cup salad leaves)<br>1 piece fresh fruit<br>8 oz low-fat yogurt | 7 oz chicken: marinated chicken breast in Five-spice Chinese marinade (see p 123) grilled or barbecued (see p 201)<br>2 cups salad with 1½ tbsp cashews & oil-free salad dressing |
| day 5 | 1½ oz high-fiber breakfast cereal with 8 oz low-fat milk<br>1 piece fresh fruit | Turkey roll (1 whole grain bread roll [2.5 oz] with 3.5 oz turkey, cranberry sauce & ½ cup salad leaves)<br>Greek Salad (see p 101) | 7 oz fish: Seared Tuna with Asian Greens & Soy (see p 131)<br>1 piece fresh fruit |
| day 6 | 2 slices whole grain raisin toast with 2 tsp light margarine<br>1 low-fat cafe latte or low-fat cappuccino | 1 slice whole grain toast with 3.5 oz sardines<br>1½ cups salad with oil-free salad dressing<br>1 piece fresh fruit | 7 oz lamb: 1 dinner serving Warm Salad of Moroccan Lamb with Roasted Tomatoes (see p 108)<br>Fresh Fruit Salad (see p 182) with 8 oz low-fat yogurt |
| day 7 | 2 eggs (poached, boiled or scrambled), with ½ tomato pan-fried in 1 tsp oil<br>1 slice whole grain toast with 1 tsp light margarine | Cheese & salad sandwich (2 slices whole grain bread with 1 oz low-fat ricotta, slices of cucumber & ½ cup salad leaves)<br>1 piece fresh fruit | 7 oz beef: grilled or barbecued sirloin steaks (see p 201)<br>Stuffed Peppers (see p 179)<br>5 oz drained canned fruit with 8 oz low-fat yogurt |

• see pages 203–7 for weekly shopping lists
note: if on 3 dairy servings (see page 22), use 1½ oz protein plus 1 extra dairy option

week ten

| | breakfast | lunch | dinner |
|---|---|---|---|
| day 1 | 1½ oz high-fiber breakfast cereal with 8 oz low-fat milk<br>1 piece fresh fruit | Roast beef sandwich (2 slices rye bread with 2 tsp light margarine, 3.5 oz rare roast beef, horseradish, slices of pepper & ½ cup salad leaves)<br>1 piece fresh fruit | 7 oz fish: marinated white fish filets in Greek-style marinade (see p 124) grilled or barbecued (see p 201)<br>2 cups steamed zucchini & carrots<br>8 oz low-fat dairy dessert |
| day 2 | 1 slice whole grain toast with 1 tsp light margarine & 2 oz grilled bacon<br>1 piece fresh fruit<br>8 oz low-fat yogurt | Ham & cheese toasted sandwich (2 slices whole grain bread with 2 oz ham, 2 oz low-fat cheese & slices of tomato)<br>1½ cups salad with 1.5 oz avocado | 7 oz beef: 1 dinner serving Poached Beef Salad with Vietnamese Dressing (see p 107)<br>1 piece fresh fruit |
| day 3 | 1½ oz high-fiber breakfast cereal with 8 oz low-fat milk & 2 tbsp dried fruit | Salmon salad (3.5 oz canned salmon, ½ cup salad vegetables, 1 oz low-fat cheese & 1 tbsp oil-free mayonnaise)<br>4 whole grain crispbreads with 2 tsp light margarine | 7 oz chicken: Chicken Stir-fry with Broccoli & Peppers (see p 141)<br>½ cup steamed bok choy<br>8 oz low-fat yogurt<br>1 piece fresh fruit |
| day 4 | 1 slice whole grain toast with ⅓ cup baked beans<br>1 piece fresh fruit<br>8 oz low-fat yogurt | Open chicken & salad sandwich (1 slice whole grain bread with 3.5 oz skinless cooked chicken, 1 tbsp oil-free mayonnaise, bean sprouts, 1 oz cheese & ½ cup salad leaves) | 7 oz lamb: Greek-style Lamb Kebabs with Tzatziki (see p 164)<br>2 cups zucchini, tomato & onion tossed in 2 tsp olive oil & grilled or barbecued<br>5 oz drained canned fruit |
| day 5 | 1½ oz high-fiber breakfast cereal with 8 oz low-fat milk<br>1 piece fresh fruit | Open Steak Sandwich (see p 152) without avocado<br>1 cup salad with oil-free salad dressing<br>1 piece fresh fruit | 7 oz fish: Swordfish Steaks with Warm Zucchini & Olive Salad (see p 128)<br>8 oz low-fat dairy dessert |
| day 6 | 1 whole grain English muffin with 1 tsp light margarine & low-calorie jam<br>Banana Smoothie (see p 182) | Ploughman's lunch (3.5 oz sliced cold meats, 1 oz sliced low-fat cheese, cherry tomatoes, slices of pickle, pickled onions & 4 whole grain crispbreads with 2 tsp light margarine) | 7 oz beef: Roast Beef with Beets, Squash & Carrot (see p 158)<br>½ cup steamed green beans<br>Fresh Fruit Salad (see p 182) with 4 oz low-fat yogurt |
| day 7 | Scrambled Eggs (see p 112), with tomato & mushrooms pan-fried in 1 tsp oil<br>1 slice whole grain toast | Cheese & salad bagel (1 whole grain bagel with 1 oz low-fat ricotta, slices of cucumber & ½ cup salad leaves)<br>1 piece fresh fruit | 7 oz lamb: coat lamb cutlets with Lamb Rub (see p 125) & grill or barbecue (see p 201)<br>Baked Mediterranean Vegetables (see p 179)<br>1 piece fresh fruit |

• see pages 203–7 for weekly shopping lists
note: if on 3 dairy servings (see page 22), use 1½ oz protein plus 1 extra dairy option

week eleven

| | breakfast | lunch | dinner |
|---|---|---|---|
| day 1 | 1½ oz high-fiber breakfast cereal with 8 oz low-fat milk<br>1 piece fresh fruit | Open tuna & salad sandwich (1 slice whole grain bread with 2 tsp light mayonnaise, 3.5 oz canned tuna, slices of cucumber & pickles & ½ cup salad leaves) | 7 oz beef: Beef & Potato Pie (see p 154)<br>½ cup salad<br>5 oz drained canned fruit with 8 oz low-fat dairy dessert |
| day 2 | 1 cinnamon & raisin bagel with 2 tsp light margarine<br>1 piece fresh fruit<br>1 low-fat cafe latte or low-fat cappuccino | Chicken salad (3.5 oz skinless cooked chicken, 1 oz cheese, 1 cup chopped salad vegetables & oil-free salad dressing)<br>1 slice rye bread | 7 oz veal: Seeded-mustard Rack of Veal with Roasted Vegetables (see p 159)<br>1 piece fresh fruit<br>4 oz low-fat yogurt |
| day 3 | 1½ oz high-fiber breakfast cereal with 8 oz low-fat milk<br>1 piece fresh fruit | Bean salad (½ cup canned three-bean mix, 2 oz ham, 1 oz cheese, 1 cup salad vegetables & oil-free salad dressing)<br>2 whole grain crispbreads with 2 tsp light margarine | 7 oz fish: Barbecued Swordfish with Charred Mediterranean Vegetables & Olives (see p 132)<br>½ cup steamed zucchini<br>Fresh Fruit Salad (see p 182) |
| day 4 | Fresh Fruit Salad (see p 182) with 8 oz low-fat yogurt | Turkey & salad sandwich (2 slices whole grain bread with 3.5 oz turkey, cranberry sauce, 1 oz cheese, 2 oz avocado & ½ cup salad leaves) | 7 oz beef: Beef, Shiitake Mushroom & Snow Pea Stir-fry (see p 152)<br>1 cup steamed carrot & broccoli<br>⅓ cup cooked rice<br>1 piece fresh fruit |
| day 5 | 1½ oz high-fiber breakfast cereal with 8 oz low-fat milk<br>1 piece fresh fruit | Pastrami & salad wrap (1 whole grain Lebanese flatbread with 3.5 oz pastrami, 1 oz low-fat cheese, slices of tomato & ½ cup baby spinach leaves) | 7 oz fish: coat white fish filets with Mexican-style rub (see p 125) & grill or barbecue (see p 201)<br>Stuffed Peppers (see p 179)<br>1 piece fresh fruit |
| day 6 | Fruit smoothie (see p 182)<br>1 slice whole grain toast with 1 tsp light margarine | Burger (see p 156)<br>½ cup salad with oil-free salad dressing<br>1 small glass orange juice | 7 oz chicken: Chicken Breasts with Roast Tomato & Mozzarella (see p 145)<br>1 cup broccoli & carrot stir-fried in 1 tsp oil<br>Fresh Fruit Salad (see p 182) |
| day 7 | 1 Scrambled Egg (see p 112) topped with 2 oz smoked salmon & capers, with 2 toasted whole grain English muffins and ½ cup arugula & spinach leaves<br>5 oz drained canned fruit with 4 oz low-fat yogurt<br>1 small glass orange juice | | 7 oz lamb: Lamb Shanks (see p 169)<br>1 boiled potato<br>2 cups boiled green beans & cauliflower<br>8 oz low-fat dairy dessert |

• see pages 203–7 for weekly shopping lists
note: if on 3 dairy servings (see page 22), use 1½ oz protein plus 1 extra dairy option

week twelve

| | breakfast | lunch | dinner |
|---|---|---|---|
| day 1 | 1½ oz high-fiber breakfast cereal with 8 oz low-fat milk<br>1 piece fresh fruit | Ham & salad sandwich (2 slices whole grain bread with 2 tsp light margarine, 3.5 oz ham, slices of tomato & ½ cup salad leaves)<br>1 piece fresh fruit | 7 oz fish: coat white fish filets with Lemon Pepper rub (see p 125) & grill or barbecue (see p 201)<br>2 cups salad with oil-free salad dressing<br>8 oz low-fat dairy dessert |
| day 2 | 1 slice whole grain toast with 1 tsp light margarine & low-calorie jam<br>1 piece fresh fruit<br>1 low-fat cafe latte or low-fat cappuccino | Egg & salad sandwich (2 slices rye bread with 2 tsp oil-free mayonnaise, 2 hard-boiled eggs, slices of onion & ½ cup salad leaves)<br>8 oz low-fat yogurt | 7 oz lamb: Rosemary & Lemon Lamb Cutlets with Baked Fennel & Red Onion (see p 162)<br>1 cup steamed green beans<br>1 piece fresh fruit |
| day 3 | 1½ oz high-fiber breakfast cereal with 8 oz low-fat milk<br>1 piece fresh fruit | Roast beef wrap (1 whole grain Lebanese flatbread with 2 tsp light margarine, 3.5 oz rare roast beef, horseradish, bean sprouts & ½ cup arugula leaves)<br>8 oz low-fat yogurt | 7 oz chicken: Poached Chicken Breast with Soy, Ginger & Shallots (see p 141)<br>2 cups broccoli, carrot & green beans, stir-fried in 2 tsp oil<br>1 piece fresh fruit |
| day 4 | 1½ cup muesli with 8 oz low-fat yogurt & 1 piece fresh fruit | Open ham & salad sandwich (1 slice whole grain bread with 1 tsp light margarine, 2 oz ham, chutney, slices of tomato & ½ cup salad leaves)<br>8 oz low-fat milk with cocoa & Equal | 7 oz lamb: Indian Lamb & Spinach Curry (see p 166)<br>1 cup steamed zucchini & carrot<br>⅓ cup cooked rice<br>1 piece fresh fruit |
| day 5 | 1½ oz high-fiber breakfast cereal with 8 oz low-fat milk | Open Steak Sandwich (see p 152) without avocado<br>½ cup salad with oil-free salad dressing<br>1 piece fresh fruit | 7 oz fish: Cajun Fish Filets (see p 131)<br>1½ cups steamed peas, carrot & cauliflower<br>1 piece fresh fruit<br>4 oz low-fat dairy dessert |
| day 6 | 1 piece fresh fruit<br>8 oz low-fat yogurt | Light Vegetable Soup (see p 94)<br>2 slices whole grain toast with 2 tsp light margarine & 3.5 oz sardines<br>1 piece fresh fruit | 7 oz beef: Beef Provençal Casserole (see p 156)<br>½ cup steamed snow peas<br>1 boiled potato<br>8 oz low-fat yogurt |
| day 7 | 1 slice whole grain toast with tomato & mushrooms pan-fried in 2 tsp oil<br>Fruit smoothie (see p 182) | Tuna salad (3.5 oz canned tuna, 1 oz feta, canned corn, chopped tomato & green beans and ½ cup salad leaves with oil-free salad dressing)<br>1 whole grain bread roll (2.5 oz) | 7 oz lamb: Roast Leg of Lamb with Rosemary & Garlic (see p 171)<br>1 baked potato<br>1½ cups boiled Brussels sprouts<br>1 piece fresh fruit |

• see pages 203–7 for weekly shopping lists
note: if on 3 dairy servings (see page 22), use 1½ oz protein plus 1 extra dairy option

# part three

## recipes for the Total Wellbeing Diet

The following recipes have been written and tested by professionals to ensure they are well within the parameters of the Total Wellbeing Diet.

Each chapter offers great variety and choice. And for the days when cooking a full meal is just too much, turn to the Sauces, Marinades & Rubs chapter for inspiration.

The quantity of food groups has been carefully calculated for each recipe and is provided at the bottom of the recipe. Use this information when planning your own daily and weekly menu plans—in much the same way as we have done in Part 2 (see pages 65–87).

Soups make a very easy and quick meal or snack, and can be as hearty or simple as you like. The following recipes use lots of lovely fresh ingredients and can be made ahead of time and stored in the fridge or frozen for use at a later date.

# soups

# butternut squash & cilantro soup

Serves 4 for lunch

3 cups good-quality chicken stock

1 cup water

1 x 2 lb butternut squash, peeled and roughly chopped

1 large onion, roughly chopped

2 carrots, roughly chopped

3 sticks celery, roughly chopped

2 cloves garlic

1 teaspoon paprika

½ teaspoon turmeric

½ teaspoon ground coriander

½ teaspoon ground nutmeg

1 cup cilantro leaves

In a large saucepan, bring chicken stock and water to a boil. Add vegetables and spices and bring back to a boil. Reduce heat and simmer for 20 minutes, or until vegetables are soft.

Allow to cool, then puree using a blender or hand-held processor. Season to taste.

Reheat soup. Serve topped with cilantro.

1 serving = 1 unit vegetables

# roast red pepper & tomato soup

Serves 4 for lunch

2 red peppers, halved and seeded

2 tablespoons olive oil

1 large onion, finely sliced

2 cloves garlic, crushed

1 tablespoon tomato paste

1½ lbs ripe tomatoes, roughly chopped

2 cups vegetable stock

1 packet Equal (optional)

1 handful basil, torn

Preheat oven to 350°F.

Place peppers in a shallow baking dish skin-side up and drizzle with half the oil. Roast for 25 minutes, or until softened. Remove from oven, then cover with foil and allow to cool slightly. Peel off and discard skin and roughly chop flesh.

Heat remaining oil in a large saucepan over medium heat. Add onion and sauté until soft. Add garlic and tomato paste and cook for 2 minutes, stirring constantly. Add peppers, tomato and stock, then cover and simmer for 15 minutes.

Allow to cool slightly, then puree using a blender or hand-held processor. Season to taste. For a sweeter soup add Equal.

Reheat soup and serve sprinkled with basil.

1 serving = 1 unit vegetables, 2 units fats

butternut squash & cilantro soup

roast red pepper & tomato soup

# light vegetable soup

Serves 4 for lunch

4¼ cups good-quality vegetable stock

2 carrots, sliced

2 sticks celery, chopped

1 onion, chopped

¼ cup roughly chopped parsley

1 x 14 oz can crushed tomatoes

¼ cup finely shredded basil

1 tablespoon rosemary, finely chopped

Bring stock to a boil in a large saucepan. Add carrot, celery, onion, parsley and tomato and simmer gently for 30 minutes.

Stir in basil and rosemary and season to taste.

1 serving = 1 unit vegetables

## variation
### beef soup
To make beef soup, add 14 oz diced beef with the vegetables, parsley and tomato. Simmer for 1 hour, or until beef is tender.

1 serving = 1 unit protein, 1 unit vegetables

# beautiful borscht

Serves 4 for lunch

4 beets, peeled and quartered

1 carrot, roughly chopped

1 parsnip, roughly chopped

1 leek, roughly chopped and washed

1 onion, roughly chopped

3 bay leaves

½ teaspoon allspice

½ cup lemon juice

6¼ cups vegetable stock

2 tablespoons low-fat natural yogurt

1 handful flat-leaf (Italian) parsley, roughly chopped

Bring vegetables, bay leaves, allspice, lemon juice and stock to a boil in a large saucepan. Reduce heat and simmer for 45 minutes.

Allow to cool slightly, then remove bay leaves and puree using a blender or hand-held processor. Season to taste.

Gently reheat soup and serve with a dollop of low-fat yogurt and a sprinkling of parsley. This soup can also be served cold.

1 serving = ½ unit vegetables

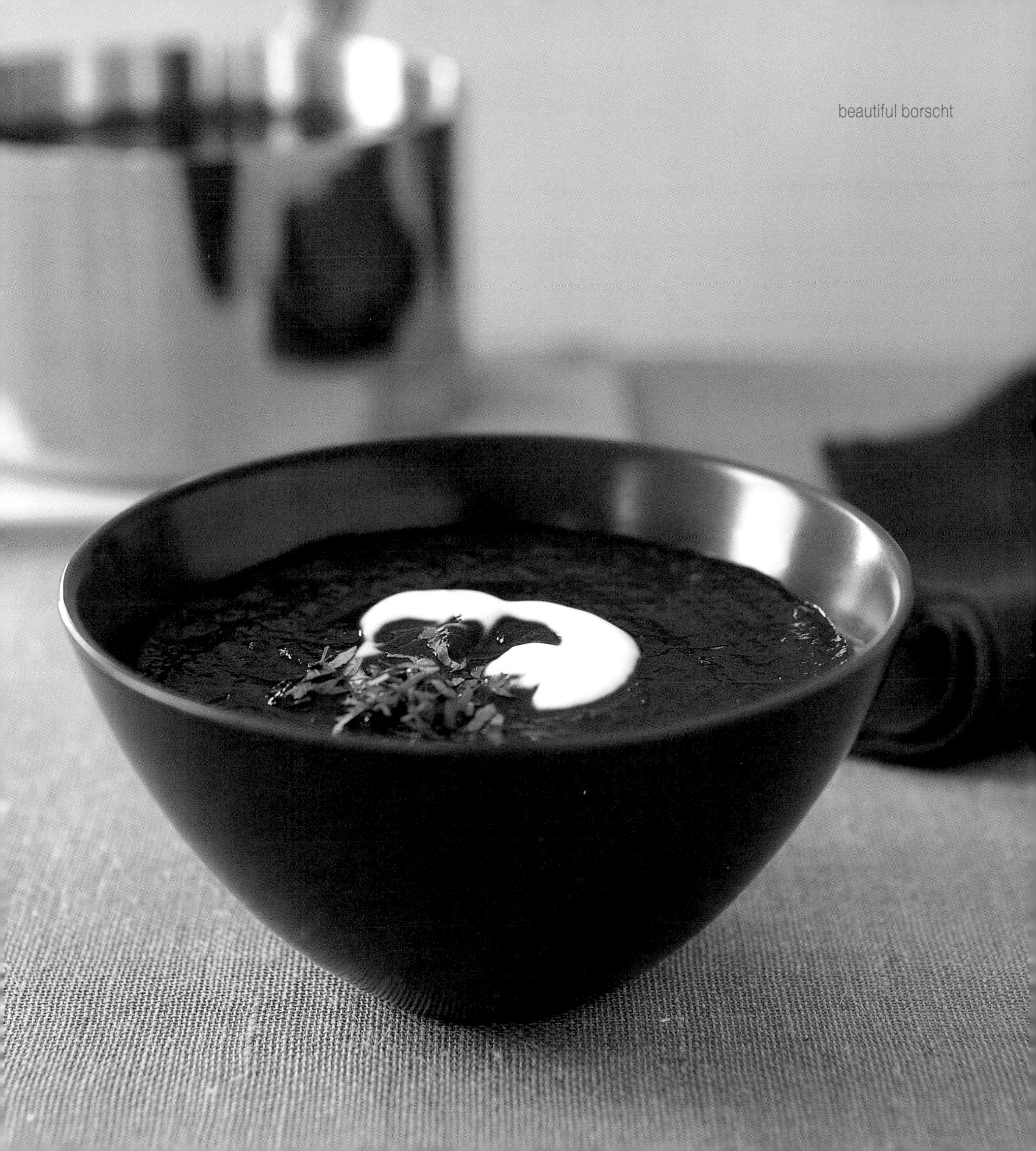

beautiful borscht

oriental chicken soup

minestrone with meatballs

# oriental chicken soup

Serves 4 for lunch

2 teaspoons peanut oil

2 stalks lemongrass, chopped (or 2 teaspoons lemongrass paste)

4 scallions, chopped

1 red chili pepper, sliced

4¼ cups good-quality chicken stock

1 tablespoon fish sauce

1 tablespoon soy sauce

14 oz chicken breast, thinly sliced

2 cups bean sprouts

1 teaspoon Equal

chopped cilantro and mint

Heat oil in a small frying pan over medium heat. Add lemongrass, scallion and chili pepper and cook, stirring, for 2 minutes. Remove from heat and set aside.

In a medium saucepan, bring stock to a boil. Add lemongrass mixture, fish sauce, soy sauce and chicken, then reduce heat and simmer for 10 minutes, or until chicken is cooked.

Add bean sprouts and stir to heat through. Season to taste with Equal—the sweetness will balance out the flavors of the soup. Serve topped with cilantro and mint.

1 serving = 1 unit protein, ½ unit vegetables

# minestrone with meatballs

Serves 4 for lunch

MEATBALLS

½ onion, finely chopped

14 oz lean minced (ground) beef

2 tablespoons finely chopped flat-leaf (Italian) parsley

1 clove garlic, crushed

2 teaspoons olive oil


SOUP

2 teaspoons olive oil

1 clove garlic, crushed

½ onion, chopped

1 stick celery, chopped

1 carrot, chopped

2 x 14 oz cans chopped tomatoes

1 cup beef stock

½ cup basil, chopped

To make meatballs, mix all ingredients except oil in a large bowl. Roll tablespoonfuls of mixture into balls and set aside. Heat oil in a large frying pan over high heat. Carefully add half the meatballs and cook, turning occasionally, for 8–10 minutes, or until browned. Remove from pan and drain on paper towel. Repeat with remaining uncooked meatballs. Do not overcrowd pan when cooking or meatballs will stew.

For the soup, heat oil in a large saucepan over medium heat. Add garlic, onion, celery and carrot and cook, stirring constantly, until onion is soft. Add tomato and stock and bring to a boil. Reduce heat and simmer, covered, for 10 minutes.

Add meatballs to soup and simmer, uncovered, for 3 minutes, or until meatballs are heated through. Stir in basil and season to taste.

1 serving = 1 unit protein, ½ unit vegetables, 1 unit fats

The Total Wellbeing Diet encourages us to eat large quantities of salad and vegetables. The following recipes are mostly lunch servings, but these can easily be converted to dinner servings by doubling the amount of protein.

# salads

greek salad

tuna with cannellini bean & basil salad

# greek salad

Serves 4 for lunch

1 head romaine lettuce, torn into large pieces

2 Lebanese (short) cucumbers, roughly chopped

1 green pepper, seeded and finely chopped

12 kalamata olives

4 Roma (plum) tomatoes, quartered

½ red (Spanish) onion, thinly sliced

2 tablespoons olive oil

1 tablespoon lemon juice

8 oz low-fat feta

Put lettuce, cucumber, pepper, olives, tomato and onion into a large salad bowl. Add oil and lemon juice and toss. Season to taste.

Crumble feta over top and serve.

1 serving = 1 unit dairy, 1 unit vegetables, 2 units fats

# tuna with cannellini bean & basil salad

Serves 4 for lunch

1 tablespoon pine nuts

4 x 3.5 oz tuna steaks

olive oil spray

1 tablespoon lemon juice

1 tablespoon olive oil

½ clove garlic, crushed

1 x 14 oz can white cannellini beans, drained and rinsed

½ cup basil, finely sliced

⅓ cup flat-leaf (Italian) parsley, finely chopped

¼ cup finely sliced scallions

Heat a small nonstick frying pan over medium heat. Add pine nuts and toss for 5 minutes, or until toasted and golden. Set aside.

Lightly spray tuna steaks with oil spray. Heat a large nonstick frying pan or grill plate over high heat until almost smoking. Add tuna and cook for 2 minutes each side—the tuna should still be pink and "glassy" in the middle (don't be tempted to cook the tuna any longer or it will be dry and unpleasant). Allow to cool slightly.

Place remaining ingredients and pine nuts in a bowl and gently toss. Season to taste.

Serve tuna with bean salad on the side.

1 serving = 1 unit protein, 1½ units bread, 2 units fats

# salmon salad with tarragon & caper dressing

Serves 4 for lunch

3.5 oz green beans

1 14 oz can salmon

12 cherry tomatoes, halved

4 scallions, finely sliced

1 head romaine lettuce, torn into pieces

DRESSING

1 tablespoon capers, finely chopped

1 tablespoon tarragon, finely chopped

2 teaspoons lemon juice

1 tablespoon olive oil

Bring a small saucepan of lightly salted water to a boil. Blanch beans for 5 minutes. Drain and cool under cold running water.

In a small bowl, mix all dressing ingredients and season to taste.

Drain salmon and place in a salad bowl with beans, tomatoes, scallion and lettuce. Pour dressing over salad, toss well and serve immediately.

1 serving = 1 unit protein, 1 unit vegetables, 1 unit fats

## variations

Salmon goes with many ingredients. Try the following combinations of flavors, or make up your own: canned salmon, red onion, pepper, tomatoes and lettuce; canned or smoked salmon with capers, red onion, asparagus and dill.

Canned tuna also makes a quick and easy lunch when tossed with other salad ingredients. For example, toss together canned tuna, celery, tomatoes, cucumber and lettuce and dress with oil-free salad dressing.

# tandoori chicken salad

Serves 4 for lunch

1½ tablespoons tandoori paste

2 oz low-fat natural yogurt

14 oz skinless chicken breast

3.5 oz arugula leaves

4 Roma (plum) tomatoes, thickly sliced

2 Lebanese (short) cucumbers, julienne

sprigs of cilantro

lemon wedges

DRESSING

5 oz low-fat natural yogurt

2½ tablespoons mint sauce

1 tablespoon olive oil

2 tablespoons lemon juice

Mix tandoori paste and yogurt in a bowl. Add chicken, turning to coat thoroughly. Cover and chill for anywhere from 30 minutes to overnight—the longer you leave it, the better the result.

Heat a grill plate or nonstick frying pan over high heat and cook chicken for 6 minutes each side, or until cooked through. Set aside for 5 minutes to rest. Cut into strips.

Mix all dressing ingredients in a small bowl. Place arugula, tomato and cucumber in a large salad bowl and top with chicken. Drizzle dressing over and serve with cilantro sprigs and lemon wedges.

1 serving = 1 unit protein, ½ unit vegetables, 1 unit fats

tandoori chicken salad

# warm chicken salad

Serves 4 for dinner
1 tablespoon herb mustard
1 clove garlic, crushed
juice of 1 lime
1¾ lbs chicken tenderloins
2 oz snow peas
3.5 oz arugula leaves
12 cherry tomatoes, halved
1 small avocado, sliced
⅓ cup basil, roughly chopped
½ red (Spanish) onion, finely sliced
1 tablespoon olive oil
2 teaspoons balsamic vinegar

Mix mustard, garlic and lime juice in a bowl. Add chicken, turning to coat thoroughly. Cover and chill for 30 minutes.

Bring a small saucepan of lightly salted water to a boil. Blanch snow peas for 3 minutes. Drain and cool under cold running water.

Preheat griller or a grill plate to hot. Cook chicken for 5 minutes each side. Remove from heat and set aside for 5 minutes to rest.

Place snow peas, arugula, tomatoes, avocado, basil and onion in a large salad bowl. Add oil and balsamic vinegar and gently toss. Arrange salad on serving plates, then top with chicken and serve immediately.

1 serving = 2 units protein, 1 unit vegetables, 3 units fats

warm chicken salad

thai pork & noodle salad

# thai pork & noodle salad

Serves 4 for lunch

1 x 14 oz lean pork filet
2 teaspoons peanut oil
2 tablespoons fish sauce
⅓ cup lime juice
1 teaspoon sugar
2 teaspoons chopped garlic
2 teaspoons chopped ginger
1 red chili pepper, sliced
3 kaffir lime leaves, finely shredded
1 cup bean sprouts
½ red pepper, seeded and finely sliced
1⅓ cups cooked vermicelli (glass) noodles
1 bunch mint leaves
1 bunch cilantro leaves

Heat a frying pan over medium heat. Coat pork filet with oil and cook for 12 minutes, turning to brown entire surface. Set aside for 10 minutes to rest.

Meanwhile, mix fish sauce with lime juice and sugar in a small bowl.

Thinly slice meat and place in a serving bowl with garlic, ginger, chili pepper, lime leaves, bean sprouts, pepper, noodles and mint and cilantro leaves. Pour dressing over salad and toss well.

1 serving = 1 unit protein, 1 unit bread, ½ unit vegetables, ½ unit fats

# poached beef salad with vietnamese dressing

Serves 4 for lunch

2 cups beef stock

1 star anise

2 strips orange zest

1 x 14 oz piece sirloin (approx. 2 inches thick)

5 oz mixed salad leaves

2 tablespoons shredded mint leaves

2 tablespoons shredded cilantro leaves

2.5 oz snow pea sprouts

½ red onion (Spanish), finely sliced

1 carrot, julienne

½ red pepper, seeded and finely sliced

DRESSING

1 tablespoon olive oil

3 teaspoons fish sauce

2 teaspoons rice-wine vinegar

½ clove garlic, chopped

1 x 1 inch piece lemongrass, thinly sliced

1 red chili pepper, finely sliced

Bring stock to a boil in a saucepan. Add star anise and orange zest, then reduce heat to simmer and allow to infuse for a few minutes. Add meat and bring to a boil. Remove from heat and set aside to gently cook for 15 minutes—meat should remain rare in the center—then drain and set aside.

Whisk all dressing ingredients together in a bowl. Place remaining ingredients in a bowl, then pour dressing over and toss to combine.

Slice meat across the grain into thin strips. Serve meat with salad on the side.

1 serving = 1 unit protein, 1 unit vegetables, 1 unit fats

# roast beef & beet salad

Serves 4 for lunch

4 cooked beets, peeled and quartered

2 oz parmesan, shaved

14 oz cold roast beef, finely sliced

generous amount of salad greens (baby spinach, arugula, romaine, etc.)

½ cup basil, torn

DRESSING

2 tablespoons olive oil

1 tablespoon balsamic vinegar

1 clove garlic, chopped

½ teaspoon Equal

1 teaspoon Dijon mustard

In a small bowl, whisk together all dressing ingredients.

Toss remaining ingredients together in a large bowl. Pour dressing over, toss and season to taste.

1 serving = 1 unit protein, ½ unit dairy, 1 unit vegetables, 2 units fats

# thai beef salad

Serves 4 for dinner

1¾ lbs rump steak

1 tablespoon olive oil

3.5 oz baby spinach leaves

1 red pepper, seeded and finely sliced

1½ cups bean sprouts

4 scallions, finely sliced

½ cup cilantro leaves

2 tablespoons chopped mint

DRESSING

2 tablespoons lime juice

1 tablespoon fish sauce

1 tablespoon soy sauce

1 clove garlic, crushed

1 red chili pepper, seeded and chopped

Heat a grill plate or barbecue grill to hot.

Brush meat with oil and cook for 3–4 minutes each side for medium-rare, or until cooked to your liking. Place steaks in a warm place, or cover with foil, and set aside for 5 minutes to rest.

Meanwhile, mix all dressing ingredients in a small bowl.

Slice meat across the grain into thin strips.

Place beef and remaining ingredients in a large bowl. Pour dressing over salad, then toss gently and serve immediately.

1 serving = 2 units protein, 1 unit vegetables, 1 unit fats

# warm salad of moroccan lamb with roasted tomatoes

Serves 4 for lunch

4 ripe Roma (plum) tomatoes

freshly ground black pepper

2 teaspoons mild paprika

1 clove garlic, crushed

1 teaspoon ground cumin

1 teaspoon garam masala

1 tablespoon olive oil

14 oz lamb steaks

1 red (Spanish) onion, sliced

1 Lebanese (small) cucumber, sliced

3.5 oz arugula leaves

DRESSING

1 tablespoon olive oil

1 tablespoon balsamic vinegar

2 tablespoons lemon juice

freshly ground black pepper

Preheat oven to 350°F. Line a baking tray with baking paper.

Slice tomatoes lengthways and remove seeds. Place tomatoes, cut-side up, on prepared baking tray and season with pepper. Roast for 20 minutes. Remove from oven and allow to cool.

In a bowl, mix paprika, garlic, cumin, garam masala and oil.

Heat a grill plate or barbecue grill to hot. Dip meat into spice mixture, coating evenly, then cook for 2 minutes each side for medium, or until cooked to your liking. Place steak in a warm place, or cover with foil, and set aside for 5 minutes to rest.

In a small bowl, whisk all dressing ingredients together. Place onion, cucumber and arugula leaves in a bowl. Add dressing and toss to combine.

Layer salad on serving plates with lamb and roasted tomatoes.

1 serving = 1 unit protein, 1 unit vegetables, 2 units fats

thai beef salad

warm salad of moroccan lamb with roasted tomatoes

Eggs are an excellent source of protein, and an important part of the Total Wellbeing Diet. This chapter shows you how easy it is to whip up quick and tasty meals using eggs—one of the most versatile ingredients.

# eggs & things

# scrambled eggs

Serves 4 for breakfast/lunch
8 eggs
7 oz low-fat milk
¼ cup chopped flat-leaf (Italian) parsley

In a small bowl, lightly whisk eggs and milk together and lightly season.

Heat a nonstick frying pan over medium heat. Pour in egg mixture and cook, repeatedly dragging the cooked egg to the center and tilting the pan to allow uncooked egg to run to the sides, until all the egg is cooked.

Sprinkle with parsley and serve immediately.

1 serving = 1 unit protein

# 2-egg omelette

Serves 1 for dinner
2 eggs
1 tablespoon cold water
2 teaspoons olive oil
3.5 oz shaved lean ham
¼ zucchini, finely sliced
2 teaspoons finely chopped flat-leaf (Italian) parsley
1 scallion, finely sliced

Lightly beat eggs with water in a small bowl.

Heat oil in a nonstick frying pan over high heat. Pour in eggs and tilt pan so eggs cover base. Cook for 2 minutes, or until mixture just begins to set.

Place ham and zucchini in an even layer on top of egg mixture. Continue to cook until omelette has set. Sprinkle over parsley and scallion and lightly season. Fold omelette in half and serve immediately.

1 serving = 2 units protein, 2 units fats

## variations
Omelettes make a wonderful base for almost any ingredient. Experiment with roasted squash, leek and thyme; red onion, pepper and basil; smoked salmon, chives and spinach; or stick with the more traditional tomato and bacon.

scrambled eggs

squash & spinach frittata

# squash & spinach frittata

Serves 4 for lunch
14 oz squash, peeled and cut into 1¼ inch cubes
1 tablespoon olive oil
1 teaspoon soy sauce
2 leeks, finely sliced and washed
2 cloves garlic, crushed
10 oz baby spinach leaves
freshly ground black pepper
8 eggs
14 oz low-fat natural yogurt
2 oz matured cheese, grated

Preheat oven to 330°F. Grease a small baking dish with a little oil.

Place squash in a bowl with 1 teaspoon oil and soy sauce and toss to coat. Tip squash onto a baking tray and roast for 25 minutes.

Heat remaining oil in a frying pan over medium heat. Add leek and cook for 5 minutes, or until soft. Add garlic and spinach leaves and cook until spinach has wilted. Tip mixture onto work surface and chop roughly. Season to taste with pepper.

Whisk eggs, yogurt and cheese together lightly in a large bowl. Add squash and spinach mixture and gently stir to combine. Pour mixture into prepared dish and bake in oven for 20 minutes, or until set. Serve with a salad.

1 serving = 1 unit protein, 1 unit dairy, 2 units vegetables, 1 unit fats

# ham & vegetable frittata

Serves 4 for lunch
8 eggs, lightly beaten
½ cup low-fat milk
4 scallions, finely sliced
1 small zucchini, sliced
8 cherry tomatoes, halved
4 mushrooms, sliced
14 oz lean ham (or cooked chicken)
1 tablespoon chopped basil
2 tablespoons grated parmesan
freshly ground black pepper

Preheat oven to 330°F. Lightly grease an 8-inch ovenproof baking dish with a little oil.

In a large bowl, whisk eggs with milk. Add remaining ingredients and stir to mix well.

Pour mixture into baking dish and bake for 35–40 minutes, or until set. Serve with a green salad.

1 serving = 2 units protein, 1 unit vegetables

# french toast

Serves 4 for breakfast
4 eggs
⅓ cup low-fat milk
1 teaspoon ground cinnamon
4 slices whole grain bread
olive oil spray
fresh strawberries

In a shallow bowl, lightly beat eggs with milk and cinnamon. Add 1 slice of bread to bowl and soak thoroughly in egg mixture.

Meanwhile, spray a nonstick frying pan with oil and heat over medium heat. Add soaked bread to pan and cook each side for 30 seconds, or until lightly browned. Repeat with remaining bread and egg mixture.

Serve sprinkled with a little extra ground cinnamon and with fresh strawberries from your daily fruit allowance.

1 serving = ½ unit protein, 1 unit bread, 1 unit fruit

# baked potato with ham, rosemary & cheddar

Serves 1 for lunch
1 large baking potato
3.5 oz lean ham, chopped
1 teaspoon finely chopped rosemary
2 scallions, finely sliced
1 oz cheese, grated

Preheat oven to 400°F.

Wrap potato in foil and bake on oven rack for 35–40 minutes, or until soft when lightly squeezed.

Remove foil and cut potato in half. With a teaspoon, scoop potato flesh into a bowl. Add ham, rosemary, scallion and cheese (reserving a little cheese for later) and mix well. Spoon ham and potato mixture back into potato skins, then sprinkle with reserved cheese. Place on a baking tray and bake for 10 minutes, or until cheese has melted. Serve with a crisp salad.

1 serving = 1 unit protein, 1½ units bread, 1 unit dairy

## variations
Baked potatoes make a wonderfully easy dinner when there isn't much in the pantry. Have a rummage in the cupboard and see what you can find—you'll be surprised how much of it goes well with a baked potato. Here are a few suggestions to get you started: caramelized onion and low-fat feta; lean bacon, rosemary and arugula leaves; poached chicken, leek and fresh herbs; or tuna, lemon and scallion.

french toast

We are lucky to have a wide and excellent-quality range of fresh meat and fish in our supermarkets and butcher shops. When contemplating meat for lunch or dinner, often nothing more is needed than adding a few spices or a simple marinade, and throwing the meat on the barbecue or grill. It really is as simple as that.

# sauces, marinades & rubs

# sauces

How long is a piece of string? The number of sauces in cooking is just about infinite, and everyone has their particular favorite. Here are a number of commonly used sauces that are delicious and well within the parameters of the Total Wellbeing Diet.

## olive tapenade

Makes about 1½ cups
1 bunch flat-leaf (Italian) parsley
grated zest of 1 lemon
juice of ½ lemon
2 cloves garlic
3.5 oz pitted green olives
¼ cup olive oil
freshly ground black pepper

Place all ingredients except the oil and pepper in a food processor. Lightly process, then, with the motor still running, add enough oil to form a thick paste. Season to taste with pepper. Serve on top of baked fish or chicken.

1 serving (1 tablespoon) = 1 unit fats

## parsley relish

Makes about 1½ cups
1 bunch flat-leaf (Italian) parsley
6 anchovy filets
2 tablespoons baby capers
grated zest of 2 lemons
½ cup lemon juice
¼ cup olive oil
freshly ground black pepper

Place all ingredients except oil and pepper in a food processor. Lightly process, then, with the motor still running, add enough oil to form a thick paste. Season to taste with pepper. Serve cooked lamb or beef with a dollop of relish on top.

1 serving (1 tablespoon) = 1 unit fats

## yogurt sauce

Makes about 1 cup

1 cup low-fat natural yogurt
1 tablespoon chopped mint
½ clove garlic, finely chopped
2 teaspoons lemon juice
½ teaspoon ground cumin

Place all ingredients in a bowl and mix well. Season to taste. Cover and refrigerate for 10 minutes before using. If the sauce is too thick, add a little water to thin it out.

Serve with grilled lamb or chicken.

1 serving = ¼ cup

## miso sesame sauce

Makes about 1 cup

2 tablespoons sesame seeds
1 tablespoon red miso paste
1 teaspoon brown sugar
1 teaspoon grated ginger
1 tablespoon lemon juice
½ cup chicken stock

Fry sesame seeds in a dry nonstick frying pan over medium heat for 5 minutes, or until golden.

Place all ingredients in a bowl and mix well. Serve drizzled over fish, chicken or vegetables.

1 serving (¼ cup) = 1 unit fats

# red pepper pesto

Makes about 1½ cups

2 red peppers, halved and seeded
2 tablespoons olive oil
2 cloves garlic
2 oz parmesan
2 tablespoons pine nuts

Preheat oven to 350°F.

Place peppers in a shallow baking dish skin-side up and drizzle with half the oil. Roast for 25 minutes. Remove from oven, cover with foil and allow to cool slightly. Peel off and discard skin.

Place all ingredients in a food processor and blend to a smooth paste. Season to taste.

Serve with grilled lamb, beef or chicken, or use to coat lamb filets before barbecuing them.

1 serving (1 tablespoon) = 2 units fats

# tomato & chili sauce

Makes about 2½ cups

1 teaspoon olive oil
½ onion, finely chopped
1 clove garlic, finely chopped
6 tomatoes, chopped
1 red chili pepper, finely chopped
1 teaspoon raw sugar
½ cup water
1 tablespoon finely chopped flat-leaf (Italian) parsley
1 tablespoon finely chopped cilantro leaves

Heat oil in a medium-sized saucepan over low heat. Add onion and garlic and cook for 5 minutes, or until soft. Add tomato, chili pepper, sugar and water. Increase heat to medium, then cover and cook for 10 minutes.

Uncover and simmer for a further 10 minutes, or until thick.

Stir in herbs and season well. Pour sauce into a sterilized bottle or jar and store, refrigerated, for up to 2 weeks.

1 serving = ¼ cup

# marinades

Marinades can be used to tenderize or flavor meat or fish. Active agents, such as vinegar and lemon juice, tenderize meat, and work well on tougher cuts. Oil- or water-based marinades are primarily used to enhance flavor.

The following marinades are sufficient for 14 oz red meat, chicken or fish. To prepare each marinade, simply mix all ingredients in a small bowl. Place the meat in a shallow dish and pour over the marinade. Turn the meat to coat it thoroughly, then cover and refrigerate for up to 24 hours. Remove the meat from the marinade and cook as desired (see pages 200–2).

It is important not to use any leftover marinade as a sauce, unless it has been cooked in some way (for example tandoori sauce basted onto baking meat). After it has come into contact with raw meat or fish, there has been a transfer of bacteria that can be harmful to humans.

## ginger soy

¼ cup soy sauce
1 teaspoon grated ginger
2 teaspoons honey
1 tablespoon lemon juice

## chili & lime

1 teaspoon sugar
⅓ cup light soy sauce
juice of 2 limes
1 teaspoon fish sauce
½ red chili pepper, finely sliced
1 teaspoon sesame oil
1 clove garlic, crushed
1 x 1 inch piece ginger, shredded
3 scallions, finely sliced

## five-spice chinese

2 tablespoons oyster sauce
1 tablespoon hoisin sauce
1 tablespoon dry sherry
½ clove garlic, crushed
1 teaspoon five-spice powder

## thai-style

¼ cup lime juice
2 tablespoons fish sauce
1 small red chili pepper, finely chopped
1 teaspoon brown sugar
¼ cup cilantro leaves

## greek-style

¼ cup lemon juice
2 teaspoons lemon zest
1 tablespoon chopped flat-leaf (Italian) parsley
1 tablespoon chopped basil
1 clove garlic, finely chopped
2 tablespoons olive oil
2 teaspoons oregano

## tandoori

⅓ cup tandoori paste
1 teaspoon ground cumin
1 tablespoon lemon juice
8 oz low-fat natural yogurt
1 clove garlic, crushed

## seafood

1 tablespoon olive oil
2 tablespoons white-wine vinegar
2 teaspoons ground fennel
½ clove garlic, finely chopped

## beef or lamb

½ cup red wine
1 tablespoon balsamic vinegar
1 tablespoon olive oil
sprigs thyme
sprigs rosemary
1 clove garlic, crushed
2 bay leaves
2 scallions, roughly chopped

# rubs

Rubs are perhaps the quickest and easiest way to jazz up a piece of meat or fish. There is no secret trick to rubs: just choose your favorite herbs and spices and sprinkle or rub them with a little oil onto raw meat. Work the rub into the meat with your fingers to ensure the entire surface is covered. Rubs work best when the meat is then char-grilled (see page 201): be sure to oil the meat, not the hot plate, or the meat will fry rather than grill.

Most of the following recipes can be mixed by hand in a small bowl. Those with larger ingredients, such as bay leaves, may require blending in a food processor or with a hand-held processor. Using a mortar and pestle is also an excellent way to blend herbs without losing any of their freshness. Just add enough oil to moisten the rub—it shouldn't be too wet, otherwise the meat won't char-grill effectively.

Rubs do not keep: make them as you need them.

## lemon pepper

lemon pepper
thyme

## zesty

mint
lemon zest
paprika

## mexican-style

lemon zest
ground cumin
ground coriander
jalapeno pepper (or cayenne pepper)

## italian-style

oregano
thyme
basil
chopped chives
finely chopped garlic

## chicken rub

bay leaf
rosemary
lemon zest and juice
freshly ground black pepper

## fish rub

scallions
finely chopped garlic
caraway seeds
ground coriander

## lamb rub

paprika
ground cumin
ground coriander
finely chopped garlic

The recipes in this chapter celebrate one of the nation's favorite foods, seafood. Thanks to our lovely long coastlines and healthy inland waters, most of us have year-round access to diverse and fresh seafood. Try these delicious and healthy meals for dinner or for lunch, substituting the specified fish or shellfish for whatever catch is in season. An extra side salad makes a lovely accompaniment to fish, keeping a meal light but ensuring it is tasty.

# seafood

# char-grilled salmon with parsley relish, asparagus & squash

Serves 4 for dinner
14 oz butternut squash, peeled and thickly sliced
1 tablespoon olive oil
4 x 7 oz salmon filets
16 spears asparagus
4 tablespoons Parsley Relish (see page 120)
lime wedges

Preheat oven to 350°F.

Place squash in a bowl with half the oil and toss to coat. Transfer to a baking dish and lightly season. Bake for 20 minutes, or until soft and golden.

Meanwhile, heat a nonstick grill plate or barbecue grill to high. Lightly brush salmon filets with remaining oil. Place salmon on grill, flesh-side down, and cook for 4 minutes. Turn salmon and cook for a further 4 minutes. Remove from heat and set aside, covered.

Bring a saucepan of lightly salted water to a boil. Add asparagus and blanch for 2 minutes, then drain. Arrange salmon on squash slices, then top with Parsley Relish and add asparagus spears. Serve with lime wedges.

1 serving = 2 units protein, 1½ units vegetables, 2 units fats

# swordfish steaks with warm zucchini & olive salad

Serves 4 for dinner
4 x 7 oz swordfish steaks
1 tablespoon olive oil
freshly ground black pepper
lemon wedges

SALAD
2 teaspoons olive oil
2 tablespoons lemon juice
½ red (Spanish) onion, finely sliced
12 kalamata olives
1 tablespoon baby capers
3 small zucchini, thickly sliced
½ cup roughly chopped flat-leaf (Italian) parsley

To make the salad, combine oil, lemon juice, onion, olives and capers in a bowl.

Steam zucchini until tender but not mushy. Transfer immediately to onion mixture and toss to coat.

Heat a nonstick frying pan over medium heat. Brush swordfish steaks with oil and pan-fry for 2 minutes each side.

Toss parsley in zucchini salad and spoon onto serving plates. Top with swordfish and season with pepper. Serve with a wedge of lemon.

1 serving = 2 units protein, 1 unit vegetables, 1½ units fats

char-grilled salmon with parsley relish, asparagus & squash

seared tuna with asian greens & soy

# cajun fish filets

Serves 4 for dinner
2.5 oz powdered skim milk

1 cup water

1 tablespoon paprika

2 teaspoons ground cumin

1 teaspoon turmeric

1 teaspoon chili powder

1¾ lbs white fish filets (whiting, snapper, flathead, etc.)

2 tablespoons olive oil

14 oz low-fat natural yogurt

1 small cucumber, finely diced

lemon wedges

Preheat oven to 400°F. Line a baking tray with baking paper.

Mix milk powder and water in a small bowl. In a separate bowl, mix ground spices.

Dip fish filets into the milk, then roll in the mixed spices.

Heat oil in a frying pan over high heat. Rapidly fry the fish, in batches, for 2 minutes each side, or until golden. Be careful not to overcrowd the pan, as the fish will stew. Place all filets on prepared baking tray and bake for 5 minutes.

Mix yogurt and cucumber and lightly season. Serve fish with lemon wedges and yogurt sauce and with salad or vegetables.

1 serving = 2 units protein, ½ unit dairy, 2 units fats

# seared tuna with asian greens & soy

Serves 4 for dinner

4 x 7 oz tuna steaks

2 teaspoons peanut oil

2 bunches baby bok choy (pak choi), leaves separated and washed

4 scallions, finely slivered

½ cup cilantro leaves

½ cup mint leaves

lime wedges

DRESSING

2 tablespoons light soy sauce

2 teaspoons lime juice

1 teaspoon grated ginger

In a cup, mix all dressing ingredients.

Heat a heavy-based frying pan over medium heat. Brush tuna steaks with oil. Add to pan and cook for 3 minutes each side.

Meanwhile, bring a little water to a simmer in a wok. Put bok choy into a bamboo steamer and place steamer in wok. Cover wok and steam bok choy for 2–3 minutes.

Divide bok choy between serving plates and arrange tuna steaks on top. Sprinkle with scallion, cilantro and mint and drizzle the dressing over. Offer lime wedges.

1 serving = 2 units protein, 1 unit vegetables, ½ unit fats

# barbecued swordfish with charred mediterranean vegetables & olives

Serves 4 for dinner

1 red pepper, seeded and thickly sliced
1 yellow pepper, seeded and thickly sliced
2 zucchini, sliced lengthways
1 red (Spanish) onion, thickly sliced
2 tablespoons olive oil
2 cloves garlic, chopped
8 kalamata olives
2 teaspoons balsamic vinegar
1 tablespoon chopped flat-leaf (Italian) parsley
¼ cup torn basil
juice of ½ lemon
olive oil spray
4 x 7 oz swordfish steaks
lemon wedges

Preheat a grill plate or barbecue grill to high.

Place peppers, zucchini and onion in a bowl with half the oil and lightly season. Toss to coat thoroughly. Transfer to grill plate and cook, turning occasionally, for 3–5 minutes, or until charred and slightly wilted. Return vegetables to bowl. Add garlic, olives, balsamic vinegar, parsley, basil, lemon juice and remaining oil and toss lightly. Cover with plastic wrap and allow flavors to infuse while cooking the fish.

Lightly spray swordfish steaks with oil spray and lightly season. Char-grill for 2 minutes each side, or until cooked. Divide vegetables between serving plates and top with fish. Serve with lemon wedges.

1 serving = 2 units protein, 1 unit vegetables, 2 units fats

# steamed cod with scallions & soy

Serves 4 for dinner

4 x 7 oz pieces cod (or perch or snapper), skin removed
7 oz baby spinach leaves
1 tablespoon julienne ginger
3 scallions, finely sliced on an angle
2 tablespoons light soy sauce
¼ cup cilantro leaves
lime wedges

Preheat oven to 425°F.

Tear off a large sheet of foil or baking paper and lay it on your work surface. In the middle of the foil place a quarter of the spinach leaves. Place a piece of fish on top, then sprinkle with a quarter of the ginger and scallion and drizzle with 2 teaspoons of soy. Bring together the long sides of the foil and fold the edge over several times. Now fold in the short ends of the foil several times to ensure the parcel is well-sealed. Repeat this process with the remaining spinach, fish and condiments.

Gently place the four parcels in a single layer in a baking dish and bake for 15 minutes.

Open each parcel carefully and slide contents onto a warm plate. Garnish with cilantro and lime wedges. Serve with your favorite vegetables or salad.

1 serving = 2 units protein, ½ unit vegetables

## variation

Fish parcels are dead-easy and accommodate lots of different ingredients. Try this method of cooking with your favorite white fish topped with a few drops of sesame oil, a small amount of crushed black beans mixed with soy sauce, sliced ginger and a splash of dry sherry.

barbecued swordfish with charred mediterranean vegetables & olives

# baked snapper with basil, capers & tomato

Serves 4 for dinner

2 tablespoons olive oil

1 clove garlic, crushed

½ red chili pepper, finely chopped

3 scallions, finely sliced

¼ cup roughly chopped basil

1 tablespoon dried oregano

2 tablespoons capers

¼ cup white wine

4 tomatoes, seeded and roughly chopped

4 x 7 oz snapper filets

Preheat oven to 400°F.

Heat half the oil in a small saucepan over medium heat. Add garlic, chili pepper and scallions and cook, stirring, for 2 minutes, or until garlic is golden. Reduce heat to medium–low, then add herbs, capers and wine and cook, stirring occasionally, for 5 minutes. Remove from heat and stir in chopped tomato.

Heat a large nonstick frying pan over high heat. Brush fish with remaining oil and sear each side for 2 minutes. Transfer to an ovenproof baking dish and spoon sauce over fish. Bake for 6–8 minutes, or until cooked—when cooked, the flesh will flake away easily when pressed with a fork.

Serve with a green salad.

1 serving = 2 units protein, ½ unit vegetables, 2 units fats

## variation

Experiment with different ingredients in the baking dish. For example, top 1¾ lbs whiting or flathead with onion slices, chopped parsley, lemon zest and fresh thyme. Pour over white wine, or lemon juice mixed with crushed garlic, and a drizzle of oil.

# moroccan snapper filets

Serves 4 for dinner

4 x 7 oz snapper filets

1 tablespoon olive oil

freshly ground black pepper

1 teaspoon ground cumin

1 teaspoon ground coriander

½ teaspoon ground cardamom

½ teaspoon ground cinnamon

1 clove garlic, chopped

¼ cup chopped cilantro leaves

¼ cup chopped flat-leaf (Italian) parsley

juice and finely grated zest of 1 lemon

Preheat oven to 350°F

Pat fish dry with paper towel. Brush with half the oil and season with pepper. Arrange fish in a single layer in a baking dish.

In a bowl, mix remaining ingredients to a loose paste. Spread paste evenly over top of fish. Seal baking dish with foil. Bake for 10–15 minutes, or until cooked—when cooked, the flesh will flake away easily when pressed with a fork.

Serve with green vegetables or salad.

1 serving = 2 units protein, 1 unit fats

baked snapper with basil, capers & tomato

# seafood paella

1 teaspoon saffron

1 teaspoon paprika

¼ cup boiling water

2 tablespoons olive oil

2 cloves garlic, crushed

1 onion, finely chopped

3 tomatoes, roughly chopped

1 cup short-grain rice

4¼ cups chicken stock

14 oz flathead filets

5 oz uncooked shrimp, peeled

7 oz mussels, bearded and washed

5 oz calamari

5 oz peas

½ cup flat-leaf (Italian) parsley, roughly chopped

freshly ground black pepper

lemon wedges

In a small nonstick frying pan, lightly toast saffron. Transfer to a cup, then crush and add paprika and boiling water. Stir to dissolve and set aside.

Heat oil in a large heavy-based frying pan over medium heat. Add garlic and onion and cook for 5 minutes, or until soft. Add tomato and cook for 3 minutes. Add rice and cook, stirring to combine, for a further 5 minutes.

Meanwhile, bring stock to a boil in a saucepan. Add stock and saffron liquid to rice mixture, stirring well to combine. Simmer, uncovered, for 15 minutes. Place fish, shrimp, mussels and calamari on top of rice. Cover frying pan with foil and cook for a further 10 minutes. Add peas, re-cover pan, and cook for a final 5 minutes. Sprinkle paella with parsley and season with pepper. Serve with wedges of lemon and offer a green salad on the side.

1 serving = 2 units protein, 1 unit bread, ½ unit vegetables, 2 units fats

# curried perch with yardlong beans

Serves 4 for dinner

1 tablespoon peanut oil

1¾ lbs perch filets, cut into chunks

1 teaspoon sugar

½ cup chicken stock

1 tablespoon fish sauce

8 oz yardlong beans, cut into 2-inch lengths

cilantro leaves

CURRY PASTE

1 red chili pepper, roughly chopped

1 stalk lemongrass, finely chopped

1 tablespoon chopped scallion

1 clove garlic, roughly chopped

2 teaspoons finely grated ginger

2 teaspoons chopped cilantro

1 teaspoon shrimp paste

2 kaffir lime leaves

Place all curry paste ingredients in a food processor and blend to a fine paste.

Heat oil in a large nonstick frying pan or wok over medium heat. Add curry paste and fish and stir-fry for 3 minutes, turning fish carefully to coat lightly with paste. Add sugar, chicken stock, fish sauce and beans and cook for a further 5 minutes. Remove from heat and sprinkle with cilantro. Serve with rice from your daily bread allowance and steamed vegetables.

1 serving = 2 units protein, ½ unit vegetables, 1 unit fats

seafood paella

curried perch with yardlong beans

Chicken and pork are tasty meats that are easy to cook. From stir-frying to casseroling and baking, the following recipes offer numerous ways to enjoy the white meat component of the Total Wellbeing Diet. Cook these dishes for family and friends, and be sure to add healthy helpings of extra side salads or your favorite vegetables.

# chicken & pork

stir-fried ginger chicken with sesame bok choy

# stir-fried ginger chicken with sesame bok choy

Serves 4 for dinner

2 teaspoons sesame seeds
2 small bunches bok choy (pak choi), halved and washed
1 tablespoon sesame oil
1¾ lbs skinless chicken breast, cut into thick strips
1 x 1½ inch piece ginger, julienne
1 clove garlic
1 small red chili pepper, finely sliced
1 onion, quartered
½ red pepper, seeded and sliced
⅓ cup dry sherry (or Chinese rice wine)
2 tablespoons soy sauce

Heat a small nonstick frying pan over medium heat. Add sesame seeds and toss for 5 minutes, or until lightly toasted. Set aside.

Bring a little water to a simmer in a wok. Put bok choy into a bamboo steamer and place steamer in wok. Cover wok and steam bok choy for 2–3 minutes. Remove from steamer and set aside.

Heat a wok or large frying pan over medium heat. Add 1 teaspoon of the sesame oil and heat until smoking, then add chicken. Stir-fry for 6–8 minutes, or until chicken is cooked and golden. Remove from wok and set aside. Wipe out wok with paper towel.

Return wok to heat and add remaining sesame oil. When oil is smoking, add ginger, garlic, chili pepper, onion and red pepper and stir-fry for 2 minutes. Return chicken to wok. Add sherry and soy sauce and stir to combine. Add bok choy and toss.

Serve sprinkled with toasted sesame seeds and with a side serving of rice from your daily bread allowance, if desired.

1 serving = 2 units protein, 1 unit vegetables, 1 unit fats

# chicken stir-fry with broccoli & red pepper

Serves 4 for dinner

1 head broccoli, broken into florets

2 tablespoons water

2 teaspoons dry sherry (or Chinese rice wine)

1 tablespoon soy sauce

2 teaspoons cornstarch

1 teaspoon sesame oil

1 tablespoon peanut oil

1 tablespoon freshly grated ginger

½ clove garlic, crushed

1¾ lbs skinless chicken breast, cut into small pieces

1 onion, quartered

1 red pepper, seeded and sliced

Bring a small saucepan of lightly salted water to a boil. Blanch broccoli for 2 minutes. Drain and cool under cold running water.

In a cup, mix water, sherry, soy sauce and cornstarch, and set aside.

Heat a wok or large frying pan over medium heat. Add oils and, when smoking, add ginger and garlic. Cook for a few seconds, stirring constantly, then add chicken and stir-fry for 6–8 minutes, or until chicken is cooked. Remove from wok and set aside.

Add onion and red pepper to wok and stir-fry for 5 minutes, or until vegetables begin to soften. Add broccoli and toss to combine. Stir cornstarch mixture, then pour into wok and stir over high heat until sauce has thickened. Return chicken to wok and toss to combine and heat through.

Serve with rice from your daily bread allowance, if desired.

1 serving = 2 units protein, 1½ units vegetables, 1 unit fats

# poached chicken breast with soy, ginger & scallion

Serves 4 for dinner

2 tablespoons light soy sauce

1 tablespoon dry sherry (or Chinese rice wine)

1 x 1 inch piece ginger, sliced

¼ cup cilantro leaves, plus extra for garnish

5 scallions, finely sliced

4¼ cups chicken stock

4 x 7 oz skinless chicken breasts

In a large saucepan or deep frying pan, bring soy sauce, sherry, ginger, ¼ cup cilantro, two-thirds of the scallion and chicken stock to a boil.

Add chicken, then reduce heat and simmer for 12 minutes. Remove from heat but allow chicken to rest in liquid for 5 minutes. Slice chicken thickly and place on serving plate. Pour over a little poaching liquid and top chicken with extra cilantro and remaining scallion.

Serve with your favorite steamed green and rice from your daily bread allowance.

1 serving = 2 units protein

# chicken with dijon mustard & white wine

Serves 4 for dinner

4 x 7 oz skinless chicken breasts
2 ripe tomatoes, diced
zest and juice from 1 lemon
1 clove garlic, crushed
¼ cup tarragon leaves, torn
1 tablespoon Dijon mustard
¼ cup white wine
½ cup chicken stock

Preheat oven to 350°F.

Place chicken in an ovenproof baking dish and sprinkle tomato over.

In a bowl, mix remaining ingredients. Pour mixture over chicken and cover dish with a lid or piece of foil. Bake for 45 minutes.

Serve with vegetables or salad.

1 serving = 2 units protein

# tandoori chicken with garlic spinach

Serves 4 for dinner

⅓ cup tandoori paste
1 teaspoon ground cumin
1 tablespoon lemon juice
14 oz low-fat natural yogurt
1½ cloves garlic, crushed
1¾ lbs skinless chicken thigh filets, cut into 1 inch cubes
2 teaspoons olive oil
3 small onions, thickly sliced
¼ cup water
10 oz baby spinach leaves
1 cup cilantro leaves
lemon wedges
mango chutney

In a plastic container, mix tandoori paste, cumin, lemon juice, two-thirds of the yogurt and two-thirds of the garlic. Add chicken, coat thoroughly and refrigerate for 3 hours at least.

Soak 8 bamboo skewers in warm water for 30 minutes.

Preheat oven to 350°F. Line 2 baking trays with baking paper. Thread chicken pieces onto skewers.

Heat oil in a nonstick frying pan over medium heat and sauté onion until soft. Transfer to a prepared baking tray.

Increase heat to high. Add chicken skewers and cook for 2 minutes one side and 1 minute other side. Transfer to second baking tray. Bake for 6–8 minutes. Slip baking tray with onion into oven for final 2 minutes of cooking time.

Meanwhile, bring water to a simmer in a large saucepan. Add spinach and cook, stirring gently, until limp. Add remaining garlic and stir gently to combine.

Toss cilantro and warm onion to combine.

Serve wilted spinach topped with onion mixture and chicken skewers and offer lemon wedges, chutney and remaining yogurt.

1 serving = 2 units protein, ½ unit dairy, 1 unit vegetables, 1 unit fats

tandoori chicken with garlic spinach

baked yogurt chicken with tomato, mint & cucumber salad

# chicken breast with roast tomato & mozzarella

Serves 4 for dinner

4 Roma (plum) tomatoes
1 tablespoon olive oil
1 small onion, sliced
¼ cup basil
4 x 7 oz skinless chicken breasts
3 oz mozzarella, thinly sliced

Preheat oven to 350°F. Line a baking tray with baking paper.

Cut tomatoes in half lengthways. Place, cut-side up, on prepared tray and lightly season. Bake for 15–20 minutes. Remove from oven and allow to cool slightly before chopping each half into 3 pieces.

Meanwhile, heat oil in a frying pan over medium heat. Add onion and basil and cook for 5 minutes, or until onion is soft. Strain off and reserve oil, and remove onion and basil to a plate.

Return pan to heat and add reserved oil. Add chicken and cook for 6 minutes each side, or until cooked through and lightly browned on both sides.

Heat grill to medium. Divide chicken between 4 serving plates and cover meat with a layer of tomato and onion mixture. Top with mozzarella slices and place under the griller until cheese has melted and is golden.

Serve with salad or vegetables.

1 serving = 2 units protein, 1 unit dairy, ½ unit vegetables, 1 unit fats

# baked yogurt chicken with tomato, mint & cucumber salad

Serves 4 for dinner

½ teaspoon Chinese five-spice powder
1 teaspoon chili powder
2 teaspoons soy sauce
1 clove garlic, crushed
1 tablespoon olive oil
8 oz low-fat natural yogurt
4 x 7 oz skinless chicken breasts

SALAD
2 Lebanese (small) cucumbers, sliced
4 Roma (plum) tomatoes, sliced
½ red (Spanish) onion, finely sliced
¼ cup mint leaves
1 tablespoon olive oil
1 teaspoon lemon juice

In a bowl, gently fold five-spice powder, chili powder, soy sauce, garlic and oil through yogurt. Coat chicken with mixture and allow to stand at least 4 hours.

Preheat oven to 350°F. Line a baking dish with baking paper.

Heat a nonstick frying pan over medium heat. Add chicken and cook for 2 minutes each side. Transfer to prepared baking dish and bake for 6–8 minutes, or until cooked through. Remove and allow chicken to rest for 5 minutes. Carve into thick slices.

To make the salad gently toss all ingredients. Divide between 4 serving plates, then add chicken and serve.

1 serving = 2 units protein, 1 unit vegetables, 2 units fats

# chicken, tomato & rosemary hotpot

Serves 4 for dinner

2 tablespoons olive oil

1¾ lbs skinless chicken thigh filets, cut into 1¾ inch cubes

2 leeks, sliced and washed

2 carrots, finely chopped

2 sticks celery, chopped

2 cloves garlic, crushed

1 cup chicken stock

½ cup white wine

1 x 14 oz can chopped tomatoes

1 tablespoon chopped rosemary

2 tablespoons roughly chopped flat-leaf (Italian) parsley

Heat oil in a large saucepan over high heat. Add chicken in batches and cook, stirring occasionally, for 5 minutes, or until browned. Remove from pan and set aside.

Reduce heat to medium, then add leek and cook for 8 minutes, or until soft. Add carrot, celery and garlic and cook for 10–12 minutes, or until vegetables are soft. Add stock, wine and tomato and bring to a boil. Reduce heat to low, then return chicken to pan and simmer gently for 35 minutes.

Add herbs and season to taste. Serve with a mixed green salad.

1 serving = 2 units protein, 1 unit vegetables, 2 units fats

# chicken & tarragon meatloaf

Serves 5 for dinner

1½ tablespoons olive oil

1 small Granny Smith apple, peeled and diced

1 onion, finely chopped

1 clove garlic, finely chopped

1 tablespoon tarragon, finely chopped

2 slices bread, crumbled into bread crumbs

1 egg, lightly beaten

3 scallions, finely sliced

1 small zucchini, grated

1 tablespoon fruit chutney

2 lbs lean ground chicken

Preheat oven to 300°F. Lightly grease a loaf pan.

Heat oil in a large frying pan over medium heat. Add apple, onion and garlic and cook for 8 minutes, or until soft and golden.

In a large bowl, combine onion mixture, tarragon, bread crumbs, egg, scallions, zucchini, chutney and chicken. Lightly season. Spoon into prepared loaf pan and bake for 1 hour. Allow to cool in the pan, then turn out onto your work surface and cut into 5 thick slices.

Serve with salad.

1 serving = 2 units protein, ½ unit bread, 1 unit fats

# lemongrass & soy chicken with sugar snap peas & asparagus

Serves 4 for dinner

1¾ lbs skinless chicken pieces on the bone, excess fat removed

5 oz sugar snap peas

16 spears asparagus

½ cup finely sliced scallion

lime wedges

MARINADE

1 stalk lemongrass, finely chopped

2 cloves garlic, crushed

2 teaspoons grated ginger

½ cup light soy sauce

½ cup chicken stock

2 teaspoons olive oil

2½ tablespoons dry sherry (or Chinese rice wine)

Mix all marinade ingredients in a bowl. Add chicken and toss to coat thoroughly. Cover with plastic wrap and refrigerate, turning occasionally, for anywhere from 2 hours to overnight—the longer you leave it, the better the result.

Preheat oven to 350°F.

Tip chicken and marinade into a baking dish, then bake for 30 minutes, basting occasionally.

Meanwhile, bring a small saucepan of lightly salted water to a boil. Blanch vegetables for 2–3 minutes. Drain and divide between 4 serving plates. Arrange chicken on top of vegetables and brush with pan juices. Sprinkle with scallion and serve with lime wedges.

1 serving = 2 units protein, 1 unit vegetables, ½ unit fats

lemongrass & soy chicken with sugar snap peas & asparagus

fennel-crusted pork filet with parsnip & baked apple

# fennel-crusted pork filet with parsnip & baked apple

Serves 4 for dinner

1 x 1¾ lbs lean pork filet
2 tablespoons ground fennel
2 tablespoons olive oil
2 apples, quartered and cored
2 teaspoons brown sugar
2 tablespoons water
4 parsnips, peeled and cut into chunks
4 sprigs rosemary
7 oz green beans

Preheat oven to 350°F.

Remove all sinew from pork. Season well, then roll in fennel. Wrap in plastic wrap and refrigerate for 10–15 minutes.

Heat a large frying pan over high heat. Coat pork with half the oil and cook each side for 3 minutes, or until golden. Set aside, covered.

Place apples in an ovenproof dish, sprinkle with brown sugar and water and cover with foil. Set aside. Place parsnip, rosemary and remaining oil in a baking dish and toss to coat. Bake for 10 minutes.

Transfer apples in their dish to oven. At the same time, add pork to the parsnip dish. After a further 10 minutes cooking, the parsnip should be golden, the pork cooked and the apples soft.

Meanwhile, bring a small saucepan of lightly salted water to a boil. Add beans and cook for 5–6 minutes, then drain.

Turn off the oven, transfer pork to a plate and allow to rest, covered, for 5 minutes. Slice pork thickly and serve with parsnip, apple and green beans.

1 serving = 2 units protein, ½ unit fruit, 1½ units vegetables, 2 units fats

# sang choy bow

Serves 4 for lunch

1 iceberg lettuce

2 tablespoons oyster sauce

1 tablespoon soy sauce

1 teaspoon sesame oil

1 tablespoon cornstarch

½ small red chili pepper, finely sliced

1 egg, beaten

2 tablespoons olive oil

8 shiitake mushrooms, sliced

2 cloves garlic, finely sliced

1 x 1 inch piece ginger, julienne

14 oz lean ground pork

6 water chestnuts, finely chopped

2 oz dried rice noodles, soaked in hot water then roughly chopped

2½ tablespoons hoisin sauce

4 scallions, finely sliced

Discarding the outer leaves, carefully cut whole leaves from the lettuce head, trimming them to form cups.

In a bowl, mix oyster sauce, soy sauce, sesame oil, cornstarch, chili pepper and egg. Set aside.

Heat oil in a large frying pan over high heat. Add mushrooms, garlic and ginger and cook, stirring, for 1 minute. Add pork and cook, stirring to break up any clumps of meat that form, for 8–10 minutes, or until brown and cooked. Drain off any excess liquid.

Return pan to heat, then add water chestnuts and noodles and cook for 4 minutes. Stir oyster sauce mixture, then add to pan and cook for 10 minutes, or until sauce has thickened. Allow mixture to cool a little.

Place lettuce leaves on serving plates and divide meat mixture between them. Drizzle hoisin sauce over meat and sprinkle with scallion. Serve with steamed greens.

1 serving = 1 unit protein, ½ unit bread, ½ unit vegetables, 2 units fats

sang choy bow

The recipes in this and the following chapter, Lamb, focus on the important red-meat component of the Total Wellbeing Diet. These pages contain numerous recipes for both quick and slow cooking and for light and more substantial meals, all of which should be served with lots of fresh salad and vegetables on the side.

# beef & veal

# open steak sandwich

Serves 4 for lunch
4 x 3½ oz rump steaks
1 tablespoon olive oil
3½ oz arugula leaves
2 ripe tomatoes, sliced
1 small avocado, sliced
4 thick slices whole grain sourdough bread, lightly toasted
1 red (Spanish) onion, thinly sliced
1 teaspoon balsamic vinegar

Heat a large nonstick frying pan over high heat. Coat steaks with oil and cook for 3 minutes each side, or until done to your liking. You may need to do this in batches—if you crowd the pan, the steaks will stew rather than sear. Place steaks in a warm place, or cover with foil, and set aside for 5 minutes to rest.

Meanwhile, layer arugula, tomato and avocado on the toast.

Thickly slice each piece of beef and place on a sandwich. Top with onion and drizzle with the remaining oil and balsamic vinegar.

Serve with salad.

1 serving = 1 unit protein, 2 units bread, ½ unit vegetables, 3 units fats

# beef, shiitake mushroom & snow pea stir-fry

Serves 4 for dinner
2 teaspoons cornstarch
½ cup beef stock
2 tablespoons soy
1 teaspoon sesame oil
1¾ lbs sirloin, finely sliced
1 tablespoon peanut oil
1 clove garlic, finely chopped
1 x 1 inch piece fresh ginger, grated
5 oz shiitake mushrooms, halved
4 scallions, cut into 1 inch pieces
3.5 oz snow peas

In a cup, mix cornstarch, stock, soy and sesame oil.

Combine beef, peanut oil, garlic and ginger in a large bowl.

Heat a wok or large frying pan over high heat. When wok is hot, stir-fry beef mixture in batches until browned. Set aside. Add mushrooms to wok and stir-fry for 2 minutes. Add scallions and snow peas and toss to combine. Stir cornstarch mixture, then pour into wok and stir over high heat until sauce has thickened. Return beef to wok to heat through.

Serve with rice from your daily bread allowance, if desired.

1 serving = 2 units protein, 1 unit vegetables, 1 unit fats

## variations
Many, many ingredients go with beef, and almost everything can be stir-fried. Toss the following combinations in your wok: beef, garlic, ginger, pepper, chili peppers, green beans and black bean sauce; beef, garlic, basil, snow peas, broccoli and soy sauce; beef, ginger, shiitake mushrooms, baby bok choy (pak choi) and hoisin.

open steak sandwich

beef, shiitake mushroom & snow pea stir-fry

# beef & potato pie

Serves 4 for dinner
1¾ lbs lean ground beef
2 tablespoons olive oil
2 onions, finely chopped
1 carrot, finely chopped
1 stick celery, finely chopped
2 cloves garlic
1 beef stock cube
½ cup hot water
1 tablespoon flour
½ cup red wine
4 ripe tomatoes, diced
1 tablespoon chopped rosemary
2 tablespoons chopped flat-leaf (Italian) parsley
2 sweet potatoes, peeled, boiled and drained
10 oz squash, peeled boiled and drained

Coat ground beef with half the oil. In a hot pan, brown ground beef in small batches. Set aside. Heat the remaining oil in a large saucepan over medium heat. Add onion, carrot, celery and garlic and cook for 4 minutes, or until soft. Dissolve stock cube in water, then add to pan with cooked ground beef along with vegetables, flour, wine, tomato and herbs. Bring to a boil, then simmer for 25 minutes.

Preheat oven to 350°F.

In a bowl, roughly mash sweet potatoes and squash with a fork. Season to taste.

Spoon pie filling into a 4¼ cup capacity ovenproof casserole dish or 4 individual dishes. Top with mash, then bake for 20 minutes. Serve with a mixed-leaf salad.

1 serving = 2 units protein, ½ unit bread, 1½ units vegetables, 2 units fats

# meatballs in tomato & basil sauce

Serves 4 for dinner
MEATBALLS
1¼ lbs lean ground beef
2 eggs
¼ cup tomato paste
1 tablespoon dried oregano
1 onion, finely chopped
2 tablespoons chopped flat-leaf (Italian) parsley
2 tablespoons olive oil

SAUCE
1 teaspoon olive oil
1 clove garlic, crushed
2 tablespoons chopped red pepper
2 x 14 oz cans crushed tomatoes
½ cup beef stock
freshly ground black pepper
¼ cup basil, torn

To make the meatballs, mix all ingredients except oil in a large bowl. Roll tablespoonfuls of mixture into balls and set aside. Heat oil in a large frying pan over high heat. Carefully add half the meatballs and cook, turning occasionally, for 8–10 minutes, or until cooked through. Remove from pan and drain on paper towel. Repeat with remaining uncooked meatballs. Do not overcrowd pan when cooking or meatballs will stew.

For the sauce, heat oil in a small saucepan over medium heat. Add garlic and red pepper and cook, stirring occasionally, for 3 minutes, or until red pepper is soft. Add tomato and stock, then reduce heat to low and simmer for 5 minutes. Add pepper to taste, basil and meatballs and simmer for a further 8–10 minutes.

Serve with salad or vegetables.

1 serving = 2 units protein, 1 unit vegetables, 2 units fats

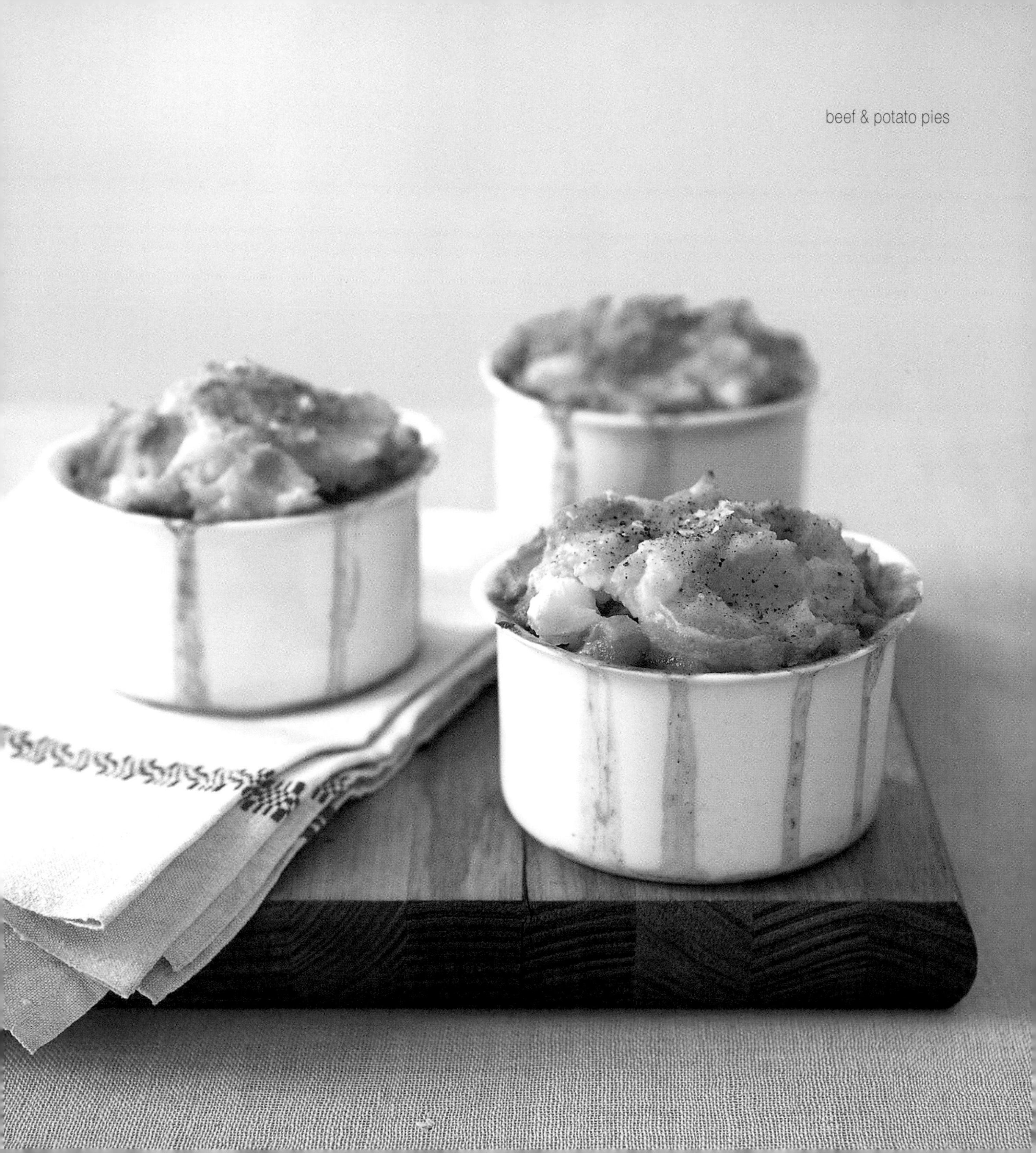

beef & potato pies

# burger

Serves 4 for lunch

4 small whole grain bread rolls

1 large ripe tomato, sliced

1 Lebanese (small) cucumber, sliced

3.5 oz salad leaves

8 slices beet (optional)

2 tablespoons ketchup (or barbecue sauce)

BURGER PATTIES

14 oz lean ground beef

½ onion

2 teaspoons dried oregano

1 tablespoon Dijon mustard

1 tablespoon tomato paste

1 tablespoon chopped flat-leaf (Italian) parsley

1 egg

Mix patty ingredients thoroughly in a large bowl. Form mixture into 4 patties. Cover with plastic wrap and chill for 10 minutes in the refrigerator.

Heat a grill plate or barbecue grill to hot. Grill patties for 6 minutes each side or until cooked through.

Meanwhile, cut bread rolls in half and top one half with tomato, cucumber, salad leaves and beets. Add a cooked burger to each and top with ketchup. Replace top half of roll and eat immediately.

Serve with a green salad.

1 serving = 1 unit protein, 2 units bread, ½ unit vegetables

# beef provençal casserole

Serves 4 for dinner

2 tablespoons olive oil

2 onions, finely chopped

7 oz field mushrooms, sliced

2 cloves garlic, crushed

14 oz diced lean beef

2 tablespoons plain flour

1 x 14 oz can diced tomatoes

1 cup red wine

1 cup beef stock

½ red pepper, seeded and sliced

1 tablespoon chopped flat-leaf (Italian) parsley

1 tablespoon chopped oregano

Preheat oven to 350°F.

Heat 2 teaspoons of the oil in a large, heavy-based frying pan over high heat. Add onion, mushrooms and garlic and sauté for 5 minutes, or until soft. Transfer to a large, ovenproof dish.

Toss meat in lightly seasoned flour. Heat remaining oil in frying pan and cook beef, in 2 batches, until well-browned. Transfer to onion and mushroom mixture.

Add tomato, wine, stock and pepper to frying pan and bring to a gentle boil, scraping up any bits of beef stuck to bottom of pan. Add to casserole dish. Cover and transfer to oven for 1½–2 hours. Remove lid and cook for a further 30 minutes, or until meat is tender. Stir in herbs and season to taste.

1 serving = 2 units protein, 1 unit vegetables, 2 units fats

# char-grilled beef filet with mushrooms & caramelized onion

Serves 4 for dinner

3 onions, finely sliced

2 teaspoons olive oil

2 teaspoons balsamic vinegar

8 field mushrooms, peeled and stems removed

½ cup white wine

1 x 1¾ lbs beef filet

3.5 oz arugula leaves

Preheat oven to 350°F.

Cook onions in oil in a saucepan over medium heat, stirring occasionally, for 30 minutes, or until soft. Add balsamic vinegar and cook for a further 5 minutes, or until mixture is sticky. Season to taste.

Heat a large nonstick frying pan over high heat and sear filet on all sides. Transfer meat to a baking dish.

Place mushrooms in a second baking dish, then pour over wine and lightly season. Cover with foil. Place both dishes in oven and bake for 15 minutes. Remove beef from oven, cover with foil and set aside to rest for 10 minutes. At the same time, remove foil from mushrooms and bake for a further 10 minutes.

Cut meat into four pieces and serve with arugula leaves, caramelized onions and mushrooms.

1 serving = 2 units protein, 1½ units vegetables, ½ unit fats

char-grilled beef filet with mushrooms & caramelized onion

# roast beef with beets, squash & carrot

Serves 4 for dinner

1 x 1¾ lbs sirloin, most fat removed

1½ tablespoons olive oil

4 carrots, cut into 1¼ inch chunks

4 beets, peeled and cut into quarters

14 oz butternut squash, peeled and cut into 4 pieces

12 cloves garlic, skins on

2 sprigs rosemary, leaves only

Preheat oven to 400°F.

Heat a heavy-based frying pan over high heat. Coat meat with 2 teaspoons of the oil and sear on all sides. Transfer to a baking dish, fat-side up. Cook in oven for 30 minutes for medium-rare, or until done to your liking.

Meanwhile, place vegetables in a separate baking dish. Drizzle over the remaining oil, lightly season, and toss to coat. Sprinkle rosemary over vegetables, then roast for 35 minutes.

Remove meat from oven, cover loosely with foil and set aside to rest for 10 minutes before carving. Serve with roasted vegetables.

1 serving = 2 units protein, 1½ units vegetables, 1½ units fats

# veal rolls in tomato & red wine sauce

Serves 4 for dinner

4 x 7 oz veal steaks, sliced

2 cloves garlic, finely chopped

2 teaspoons finely chopped flat-leaf (Italian) parsley

2 teaspoons finely chopped sage

2 teaspoons finely chopped basil

1 tablespoon olive oil

1 small onion, chopped

6 oz button mushrooms, sliced

1 tablespoon tomato paste

7 oz water

½ cup red wine

4 Roma (plum) tomatoes, diced

Place veal on chopping board, cover with plastic wrap and pound with a mallet, or your fist, to a thickness of 2 inches. Lightly season and sprinkle with garlic, parsley, sage and basil. Roll each slice of veal up tightly, and secure with toothpicks.

Heat oil in a large, deep-sided frying pan over high heat. Add rolls and cook, turning occasionally, for 6 minutes, or until browned on all sides. Remove from pan and set aside.

Add onion and mushrooms to pan and cook over high heat for 1 minute. Mix tomato paste with water then add to pan with wine and tomato. Return veal rolls to pan, reduce heat to low and cook gently for 20 minutes, or until tender. Serve with your favorite steamed vegetables.

1 serving = 2 units protein, 1 unit vegetables, 1 unit fats

# seeded-mustard rack of veal with roasted vegetables

Serves 4 for dinner

1 lb squash, peeled and roughly chopped

2 carrots, cut into thick strips

2 zucchini, cut into large pieces

4 small brown onions, halved

2 tablespoons olive oil

2 tablespoons whole grain mustard

4 scallions, finely chopped

1 teaspoon finely grated orange zest

¼ cup orange juice

3 lbs rack of veal (7 oz meat per person), trimmed of fat

Preheat oven to 400°F.

Place squash, carrot, zucchini and onions in a large, shallow baking dish, then add half the oil and toss to coat.

Mix the mustard, scallion, zest, juice and remaining oil in a bowl. Place veal on a wire rack set over vegetables, and coat meat with mustard mixture. Roast, uncovered, for 40 minutes, or until veal is cooked to your liking. Remove meat from oven, cover loosely with foil and set aside to rest for 10 minutes before carving.

Serve veal with roasted vegetables.

1 serving = 2 units protein, 1½ units vegetables, 2 units fats

seeded-mustard rack of veal with roasted vegetables

Lamb is so flavorful often nothing more is needed when cooking it than roasting a leg or frying up some chops. This chapter includes recipes for those dishes, but also introduces other ways to cook and enjoy lamb while retaining its tenderness and favored flavor.

lamb

# rosemary & lemon lamb cutlets with baked fennel & red onion

Serves 4 for dinner

3 lbs lamb cutlets (7 oz meat per person), trimmed of fat
2 bulbs fennel, sliced
2 red (Spanish) onions, cut into wedges
1 tablespoon olive oil
3.5 oz baby spinach leaves

MARINADE

2 tablespoons chopped rosemary
2 teaspoons chopped tarragon
2 teaspoons chopped flat-leaf (Italian) parsley
1 tablespoon olive oil
2 tablespoons lemon juice

Mix marinade ingredients and pour into a shallow dish. Add meat and turn to coat thoroughly. Cover and allow to marinate for 30 minutes.

Preheat oven to 350°F.

Place fennel and onion in a baking dish and drizzle with oil. Bake for 20 minutes.

Meanwhile, preheat grill plate or barbecue grill to hot. Add cutlets and cook for 1 minute each side, or until done to your liking. Set aside to rest.

Toss spinach leaves in hot vegetables and lightly season. Arrange on serving plates and top with cutlets.

1 serving = 2 units protein, 1 unit vegetables, 2 units fats

rosemary & lemon lamb cutlets with baked fennel & red onion

# spiced lamb chops with ratatouille

Serves 4 for dinner

1¾ lbs lamb loin chops, trimmed of fat
1 tablespoon olive oil
lemon wedges

SPICE CRUST
1 tablespoon freshly ground black pepper
2 teaspoons whole coriander seeds
1 teaspoon garam masala
2 cardamom pods, crushed
1 teaspoon chili powder

RATATOUILLE
2 teaspoons olive oil
4 baby eggplants, halved lengthways
1 onion, finely chopped
1 clove garlic, chopped
1 red pepper, seeded and sliced
1 zucchini, sliced
½ cup chicken stock
2 ripe tomatoes, diced
1 tablespoon chopped flat-leaf (Italian) parsley
½ cup basil, torn

To make the spice crust, mix all spices well in a bowl. Coat chops with a little olive oil, then coat thoroughly in spice mixture. Cover with plastic wrap and refrigerate for 1 hour.

To make the ratatouille, heat oil in a large frying pan over medium heat. Add eggplant and cook for 4 minutes, or until golden. Add onion and garlic and sauté until lightly colored. Add pepper and zucchini and cook for 1 minute, then add chicken stock and tomato. Bring to a boil and cook for a further 5 minutes. Add herbs and season to taste. Keep warm over heat.

Heat oil in a frying pan over high heat and cook chops for 3 minutes each side, or until done to your liking. Divide ratatouille between plates and top with chops and a wedge of lemon.

1 serving = 2 units protein, 1½ units vegetables, 1½ units fats

spiced lamb chops with ratatouille

# spiced lamb filets with broccolini

Serves 4 for dinner

2 cloves garlic
2 tablespoons olive oil
1¾ lbs lamb filets
2 onions, sliced
2 tablespoons tomato paste
½ cup red wine
1½ tablespoons raisins
½ small green chili pepper, chopped
1 tablespoon shredded mint
½ teaspoon paprika
1 tablespoon pine nuts
zest of 1 lemon
2 bunches broccolini

Place garlic and oil in a bowl. Add lamb and toss to coat thoroughly.

Heat a large frying pan over high heat. Brown lamb, in small batches, for 1–2 minutes, then remove from pan and set aside. Add onion to pan and cook for 5 minutes, or until soft. Stir in tomato paste, wine, raisins, chili pepper, mint, paprika, pine nuts and lemon zest and cook for 2–3 minutes. Return meat to the pan to heat through.

Meanwhile, bring a small saucepan of lightly salted water to a boil. Blanch broccolini for 2–3 minutes, then drain.

Top lamb with onion mixture and serve broccolini alongside.

1 serving = 2 units protein, 1 unit vegetables, 2½ units fats

# greek-style lamb kebabs with tzatziki

Serves 4 for dinner

1¾ lbs lamb filets, cut into cubes

MARINADE
2 tablespoons dried oregano
1 tablespoon olive oil
1 clove garlic, crushed

TZATZIKI
1 clove garlic, crushed
8 oz low-fat natural yogurt
1 Lebanese (small) or continental cucumber, finely grated
½ red (Spanish) onion, finely diced
1 tablespoon chopped flat-leaf (Italian) parsley
1 tablespoon chopped mint

Mix marinade ingredients in a shallow dish. Add lamb, turning to coat thoroughly. Lightly season, then cover with plastic wrap and refrigerate for anywhere from 2 hours up to overnight—the longer you leave it, the better the result.

If using bamboo skewers, soak in hot water for 30 minutes prior to use.

Preheat grill plate or barbecue grill to high.

Thread lamb onto eight skewers. Grill for 2 minutes each side—8 minutes in total—or until done to your liking.

Meanwhile, combine all tzatziki ingredients in a bowl and lightly season. Serve alongside kebabs and offer a salad.

1 serving = 2 units protein, 1 unit fats

spiced lamb filets with broccolini

greek-style lamb kebabs with tzatziki

# cilantro & chili pepper lamb kebabs

Serves 4 for dinner

1 onion, chopped
2 cloves garlic, crushed
1 bunch cilantro, roughly chopped
2 tablespoons lemon juice
2 tablespoons white wine
1 tablespoon olive oil
1 teaspoon ground coriander
1 tablespoon garam masala
2 small red chili peppers
1 teaspoon turmeric
1¾ lbs lamb filets, cut into cubes

If using bamboo skewers, soak in hot water for 30 minutes prior to use.

Place all ingredients other than meat in a food processor and blend until well combined.

Thread meat onto 8 skewers and place in a shallow dish. Pour over marinade, turning kebabs to coat thoroughly. Cover with plastic wrap and allow to marinate for at least 30 minutes.

Heat a grill plate or barbecue grill to hot. Grill kebabs for 2 minutes each side—8 minutes in total—or until done to your liking. (During cooking, brush kebabs with leftover marinade.)

Serve with a salad or vegetables.

1 serving = 2 units protein, 1 unit fats

## variations

Kebabs are a wonderful way to experiment with different meats, vegetables and marinades, since almost everything works. Choose your favorite type of meat or vegetables, turn to the Marinades, Sauces & Rubs chapter, and go for it.

# indian lamb & spinach curry

Serves 4 for dinner

2 tablespoons olive oil
2 onions, finely sliced
2 cloves garlic, crushed
½ teaspoon cardamom seeds
1 teaspoon ground cinnamon
1 tablespoon garam masala
2 teaspoons turmeric
1¾ lbs lamb leg, cut into cubes
½ cup low-fat natural yogurt
1 x 14 oz can chopped tomatoes
1 x 8 oz pack frozen spinach, defrosted
1 cup water
2 tablespoons finely shredded mint
½ cup cilantro leaves, roughly chopped

Heat oil in a large heavy-based saucepan over high heat. Add onion and garlic and cook for 5 minutes, or until onion is golden. Add spices and lamb, then mix well and cook for 6–8 minutes, or until lamb begins to cook and change color. Stir in yogurt, then tomato. Add spinach and water, then reduce heat to medium and cook for 40 minutes, or until meat is tender.

Stir in mint and cilantro and serve with rice from your daily bread allowance, if desired.

1 serving = 2 units protein, 1 unit vegetables, 2 units fats

# italian lamb casserole

Serves 4 for dinner

1¾ lbs lamb leg, cut into 1½ inch cubes

2 tablespoons olive oil

1 onion, finely chopped

1 carrot, finely chopped

1 stick celery, finely chopped

2 cloves garlic, crushed

¼ cup red wine

2 tablespoons tomato paste

2 cups chicken stock

1 bay leaf

2 sprigs rosemary

water

2 parsnips, peeled and chopped

2 tablespoons flat-leaf (Italian) parsley

Preheat oven to 350°F.

Heat a large enameled cast-iron casserole over high heat. Coat lamb with oil and cook, in small batches, for 5 minutes, or until browned. Remove from pan and set aside. Add onion, carrot and celery to pan and cook for 5 minutes, or until soft. Return lamb to pan, then add garlic, red wine and tomato paste and cook for a further 5 minutes. Add stock, bay leaf, rosemary and enough water to ensure lamb is covered. Cover with lid and bake in oven for 1 hour.

Add parsnip and cook for a further 40 minutes.

Serve sprinkled with parsley.

1 serving = 2 units protein, 1 unit vegetables, 2 units fats

italian lamb casserole

baked rack of lamb with baby vegetables

# lamb shanks

Serves 4 for dinner

4½ lbs lamb shanks (7 oz meat per person), on the bone

2 tablespoons olive oil

2 cloves garlic

2 onions, chopped

1 cup diced celery

1 cup white wine

3 cups chicken stock

1 tablespoon lemon zest

3 stalks parsley

2 bay leaves

¼ cup chopped flat-leaf (Italian) parsley

Preheat oven to 325°F.

Heat a large, enameled cast-iron casserole over high heat. Coat shanks with oil and cook, turning occasionally, for 10 minutes, or until well-browned. Remove shanks to a plate.

Add garlic, onion and celery to the casserole and cook for 5 minutes, or until soft. Add wine, stock, lemon zest, parsley stalks and bay leaves and bring to a boil. Return shanks to casserole and lightly season. Cover with lid and cook, in the oven, for 1½–2 hours, or until meat begins to fall off the bone.

Check seasoning, then garnish with parsley. Serve with steamed vegetables.

1 serving = 2 units protein, 2 units fats

# baked rack of lamb with baby vegetables

Serves 4 for dinner

1 tablespoon olive oil

4 sprigs thyme, chopped

1 tablespoon chopped tarragon

1 tablespoon chopped flat-leaf (Italian) parsley

1 clove garlic

finely grated zest of 1 lemon

3 lbs rack of lamb (7 oz meat per person), trimmed of fat

7 oz pearl (pickling) onions

7 oz baby carrots

7 oz green beans

7 oz peas

Preheat oven to 400°F.

In a bowl, mix half the oil with herbs, garlic and lemon zest.

Heat a large frying pan over high heat. Coat lamb in remaining oil and sear until golden on both sides. Transfer to a baking dish and rub herb mixture into rack. Add onions to dish and bake for 25 minutes. Remove meat from oven, cover loosely with foil and set aside to rest for 10 minutes.

Bring a large saucepan of lightly salted water to a boil. Cook carrots for 2 minutes, then add beans and peas and cook for a further 4 minutes. Drain and serve with lamb.

1 serving = 2 units protein, 2 units vegetables, 1 unit fats

roast leg of lamb with rosemary & garlic

# roast leg of lamb with rosemary & garlic

Serves 4 for dinner

1 x 3½ lb leg of lamb (7 oz meat per person), trimmed of fat

1 tablespoon olive oil

2 sprigs rosemary

2 cloves garlic, skin on and halved

2 lemons, quartered

½ cup white wine

Preheat oven to 350°F.

Rub meat with oil and lightly season. Place rosemary, garlic and lemon in a baking dish and pour in wine. Place lamb on top and bake for 1 hour.

Remove from oven, cover loosely with foil and set aside to rest for 10 minutes before carving. (This cooking time will produce pink lamb. If you prefer yours slightly more cooked, leave it in the oven for another 10–30 minutes.)

Serve with your favorite vegetables—either potato and squash, peeled and added to the baking dish 1 hour before the end of cooking time; or fresh greens, such as peas or beans, steamed, boiled or blanched.

1 serving = 2 units protein, 1 unit fats

The Total Wellbeing Diet recommends plentiful amounts of vegetables, and this chapter includes recipes for main meals as well as side dishes. Match the side dishes with other meals in the Recipe section to increase your intake of vegetables and enjoy your vegetable/salad quota each day.

# vegetables

steamed greens with toasted almonds

## steamed greens with toasted almonds

Serves 4 as a side

2 tablespoons flaked almonds
12 spears asparagus
8 oz broccoli, broken into florets
2 zucchini, chopped into 1½ inch lengths
5 oz green beans
3.5 oz sugar snap peas
2 teaspoons olive oil
1 teaspoon balsamic vinegar

Heat a small nonstick frying pan over medium heat. Add almonds and toss for 5 minutes, or until lightly toasted. Set aside.

Place asparagus in a steamer and steam for 3 minutes. Add broccoli, zucchini, beans and peas and steam for a further 5 minutes, or until all vegetables are tender. Transfer to a bowl and toss gently with oil and balsamic vinegar. Scatter with almonds and serve immediately.

1 serving = 1½ units vegetables, 1 unit fats

# sesame tofu with asian mushrooms

Serves 4 for lunch

2 teaspoons sesame seeds

14 oz firm tofu

2 tablespoons olive oil

1 cup shiitake mushrooms

1 cup enoki mushrooms

1 cup oyster mushrooms

1 clove garlic, finely sliced

¼ cup light soy sauce

¼ cup vegetable stock

½ cup finely sliced scallion

1 teaspoon cornstarch

1 tablespoon cold water

1 tablespoon chopped cilantro leaves

Preheat oven to 300°F.

Heat a small nonstick frying pan over medium heat. Add sesame seeds and toss for 5 minutes, or until lightly toasted. Set aside.

Cut tofu into 1¼ inch slices and dab with paper towel to absorb as much water as possible. Heat half the oil in a large nonstick frying pan over high heat. Add tofu and cook for 3 minutes each side, or until golden. Transfer tofu to a serving plate and keep warm in the oven.

Reduce heat to medium and add remaining oil to pan. Add mushrooms and garlic and sauté for 5 minutes, or until mushrooms are soft and golden. Add soy sauce and stock and bring to a boil. Add scallion. Mix cornstarch with water, then pour into liquid in pan and stir over heat until sauce has thickened. Add cilantro. Arrange tofu on serving plates, spoon mushroom mixture over and sprinkle with toasted sesame seeds.

1 serving = 1 unit protein, 1 unit vegetables, 2 units fats

# spiced red lentils with green beans & mint

Serves 4 as a side

1 tablespoon olive oil

1 onion, chopped

2 cloves garlic, crushed

1 tablespoon grated ginger

½ teaspoon fennel seeds

2 teaspoons turmeric

1 tablespoon garam masala

½ teaspoon cardamom seeds

1 green chili pepper, seeded and finely chopped

1 x 14 oz can diced tomatoes

14 oz red lentils, rinsed

7 oz squash, peeled and cut into 1 inch dice

1 cup water

5 oz green beans

2 tablespoons shredded mint

⅓ cup low-fat natural yogurt, to serve

Heat oil in a large saucepan over medium heat. Add onion, garlic and ginger and cook, stirring, for 5 minutes, or until onion is golden. Add spices and chili pepper and cook, stirring constantly, for 1 minute. Add tomato, lentils, squash and water (the vegetables should be covered—if not, just add a little more water), and bring to a boil. Reduce heat and simmer for 30 minutes, or until lentils are soft.

Add beans and cook for a further 3 minutes. Gently stir mint in and lightly season. Serve with a dollop of yogurt and rice from your daily bread allowance, if desired.

1 serving = 1 unit bread, 1 unit vegetables, 1 unit fats

stir-fried baby corn with snow peas

# stir-fried baby corn with snow peas

Serves 4 as a side

1 tablespoon peanut oil
1 clove garlic
1 teaspoon grated ginger
1 onion, sliced
5 oz snow peas
5 oz oyster mushrooms
12 oz Chinese cabbage, shredded
3.5 oz baby corn
2 tablespoons oyster sauce
1 tablespoon light soy sauce
2 tablespoons cilantro leaves

Heat a wok or large frying pan over high heat. Add oil and, when smoking, add garlic, ginger and onion and stir-fry for 2–3 minutes, or until onion begins to soften. Add snow peas, mushrooms, cabbage and corn and stir-fry for 5 minutes, or until almost cooked. Add oyster sauce, soy sauce and cilantro and cook for 1 minute. Serve immediately.

1 serving = 1½ units vegetables, 1 unit fats

# baked mushrooms with goat's cheese & watercress

Serves 4 for lunch

8 large field mushrooms, stems removed

8 sprigs lemon thyme

1 cup white wine

3.5 oz goat's cheese

4 scallions, finely sliced

1 tablespoon chopped basil

1 tablespoon olive oil

2 teaspoons balsamic vinegar

1 bunch watercress, washed and trimmed

Preheat oven to 350°F.

Place mushrooms, underside up, in a baking dish. Add thyme, pour over wine and lightly season. Cover with foil and bake for 15 minutes.

In a bowl, mix goat's cheese, scallion, basil and 1 teaspoon of the oil. Spoon mixture evenly onto mushrooms, then bake for a further 10 minutes.

Mix together balsamic vinegar and remaining oil. Serve mushrooms with a salad of watercress and balsamic dressing.

1 serving = 1 unit dairy, 2 units vegetables, 1 unit fats

baked mushrooms with goat's cheese & watercress

baked mediterranean vegetables with ricotta

# stuffed peppers

Serves 4 for lunch

1 tablespoon olive oil

1 small onion, finely chopped

2 cloves garlic, crushed

2 large tomatoes, chopped

12 button mushrooms, sliced

5 oz baby spinach leaves

1 egg, lightly beaten

1 tablespoon water

4 yellow peppers, halved lengthways and seeded

2 oz grated parmesan

2 tablespoons shredded basil

Preheat oven to 350°F.

Heat oil in a medium-sized nonstick frying pan over high heat. Add onion, garlic, tomato, mushrooms and spinach leaves and cook for 5 minutes, or until vegetables are soft.

Transfer to a bowl and allow to cool slightly. Add egg and water, lightly season and stir to combine. Spoon mixture into pepper shells and sprinkle tops with parmesan and basil. Place on a baking tray and bake for 15–20 minutes, or until pepper is soft and cheese is brown. Serve with salad.

1 serving = ½ unit dairy, 2 units vegetables, 1 unit fats

# baked mediterranean vegetables with ricotta

Serves 4 for lunch

1 red pepper, halved and seeded

1 yellow pepper, halved and seeded

4 zucchini, finely sliced lengthways

1 eggplant, finely sliced

1 tablespoon olive oil

1 clove garlic, crushed

2 red (Spanish) onions, finely sliced

4 Roma (plum) tomatoes, diced

½ cup torn basil

8 oz low-fat ricotta

Heat oven to 350°F.

Place peppers, skin-side up, in a baking dish and drizzle with a little olive oil. Roast for 20 minutes. Remove from oven, cover with foil and allow to cool slightly. Peel off and remove skin and slice flesh into thick strips.

Preheat grill plate or barbecue grill to high. In a bowl, toss zucchini and eggplant with half the oil. Grill vegetables until soft.

Heat remaining oil in a large nonstick frying pan over high heat. Add garlic and onion and sauté until soft.

Arrange vegetables, including tomato and basil, in layers in a nonstick baking dish, lightly seasoning every few layers. Crumble ricotta over the top and bake for 30 minutes. Allow to cool for 10 minutes before serving.

1 serving = 1 unit dairy, 2 units vegetables, 1 unit fats

Who says you can't? Fresh fruit makes healthy and refreshing drinks and desserts. Try the following recipes, experimenting with your favorite seasonal fruits.

# desserts & drinks

# banana smoothie

Serves 4

1 teaspoon Equal
4 bananas
3 cups low-fat milk
8 oz low-fat vanilla yogurt
2 teaspoons ground cinnamon

Place all ingredients in a blender and process until smooth. Divide between 4 glasses and sprinkle with a little extra cinnamon.

1 serving = 1 unit dairy, 1 unit fruit

## variations
Try smoothies made with other fruits, such as mango, apple or berries, for an alternative refreshing snack.

# fresh fruit salad

Serves 4

2 mangoes
8 strawberries
2 passion fruit
2 kiwifruit

Slice fresh fruit, toss and serve. Easy!

1 serving = 1½ units fruit

# mango & berry frappe

Serves 4

5 oz frozen berries
5 oz fresh mango
10 oz orange juice
1 tablespoon mint
ice

Place all ingredients in a blender and process until smooth. Divide between 4 glasses.

1 serving = 1 unit fruit

# poached pears with blue cheese

Serves 4

4 firm pears, peeled
2 cinnamon sticks
2 cloves
1 teaspoon allspice
1 teaspoon black peppercorns
1 bay leaf
2 cups red wine
10 oz water
4 oz blue cheese
1 teaspoon Equal

Place all ingredients except cheese and Equal into a saucepan and bring to a boil. Reduce heat and simmer for 20 minutes. Remove from heat and allow to cool slightly. Add Equal and mix well. Set aside for 4 hours.

Drain pears and serve with 1oz cheese per person.

1 serving = 1 unit dairy, 1 unit fruit

# baked custard

Serves 4

1¾ cups low-fat milk
1 teaspoon Equal
1 teaspoon vanilla
4 eggs
2 teaspoons ground cinnamon

Preheat oven to 300°F.

Heat milk, Equal and vanilla in a saucepan over medium heat. Do not let mixture boil. Allow to cool slightly.

In a bowl, whisk eggs with half the cinnamon. Slowly add milk mixture to eggs, whisking constantly. Pour into a 6 cup capacity ovenproof dish. Place dish in a deep baking dish and pour enough warm water into the dish to come halfway up sides of custard dish.

Carefully transfer to oven and bake for 35 minutes, or until just set. Sprinkle with remaining cinnamon and serve.

1 serving = ½ unit protein, ½ unit dairy

baked pineapple with vanilla yogurt & mint

# stewed rhubarb

Serves 4

12 stalks rhubarb (or 1¼ lbs other fruit), chopped into 1 inch pieces
juice and finely grated zest of 1 lemon
1 tablespoon Equal
1 teaspoon vanilla
1 teaspoon ground cinnamon
2 tablespoons orange juice
a little slivered orange zest

Place all ingredients in a deep stainless-steel frying pan. Cook over low heat for 8 minutes, or until soft. Allow to cool until just warm. Refrigerate until needed. Serve with low-fat natural yogurt.

Try stewing other fruits, varying the other ingredients to taste.

1 serving = 1 unit fruit

# baked pineapple with vanilla yogurt & mint

Serves 4

1¼ lbs pineapple, peeled and cut into chunks
2 sticks cinnamon
3 cloves
2 teaspoons brown sugar
½ cup water
3.5 oz vanilla yogurt
mint leaves

Preheat oven to 425°F.

Place pineapple, cinnamon, cloves, sugar and water in a baking dish. Cover with foil and bake for 30 minutes. Remove foil and bake for a further 15 minutes until golden and juices have caramelized. Serve with a dollop of yogurt and mint leaves.

1 serving = 1 unit fruit

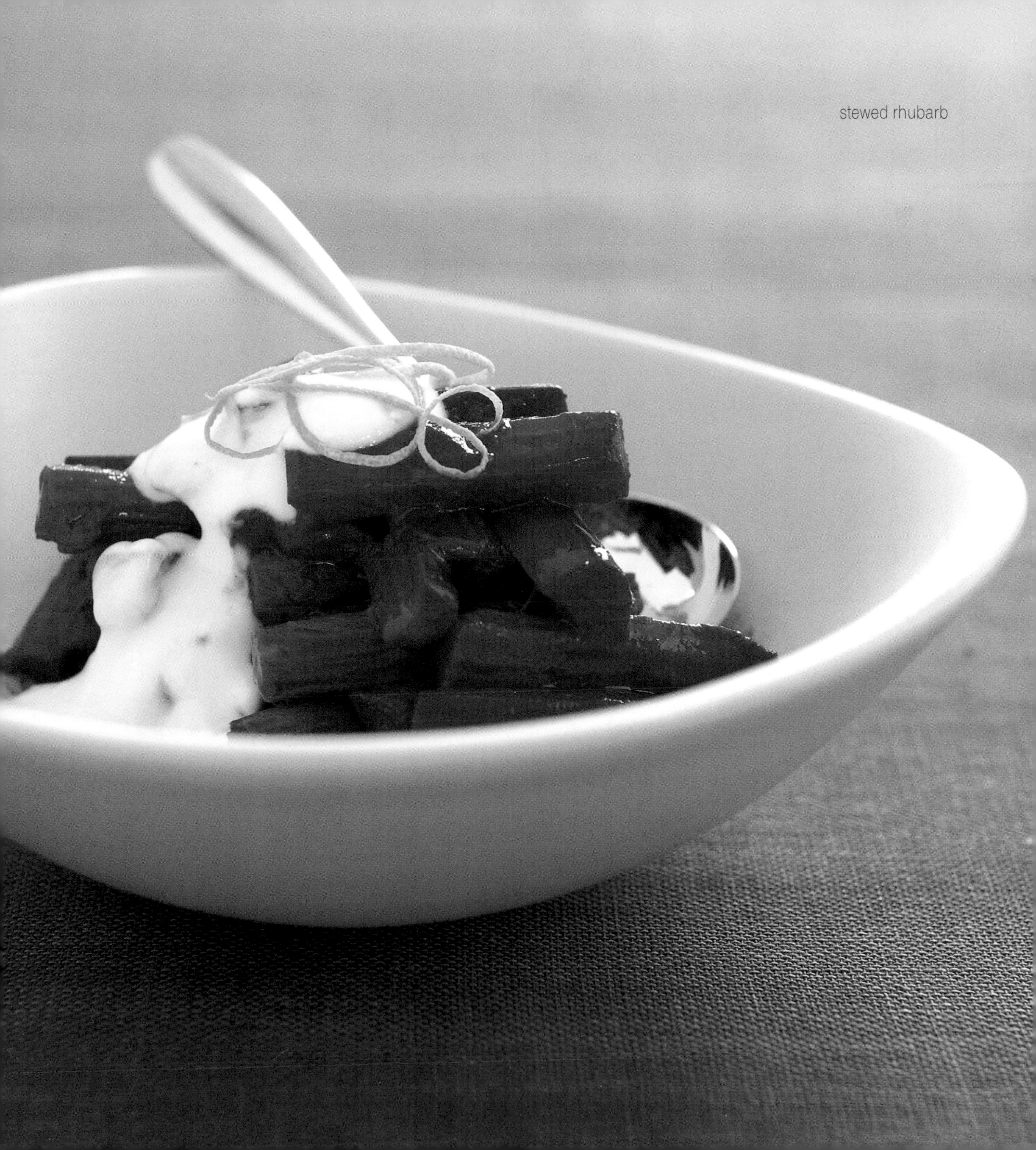

stewed rhubarb

# part four

## maintaining your new low weight

# the Total Wellbeing Diet maintenance plan

Losing excess pounds is one thing, but the real challenge is maintaining your new weight, not regaining the weight you lost. However, there are some tricks of the trade. Here are some tips to help prevent weight regain.

## keeping it off: 10 smart tactics

1   Make the commitment for life. Your new approach to healthy eating and your resolve to be more active should not end when you've lost the weight. Slipping back into tired old habits is a dieter's number one downfall. Becoming healthier and fitter is for keeps, not just a week or a month or in time for summer, so make that commitment for life and maintain control and your new weight! Check your weight each week, at the same time.

2   Be realistic. Your eating and exercise plan must fit in with your lifestyle and not be so inconvenient that you're constantly making excuses not to eat well or exercise regularly. No point signing up for yoga classes if you never attend them because they clash with the kids' after-school activities. No point choosing a diet that requires endless hours of meal preparation when you have limited time. No point choosing a plan that requires a string of exotic ingredients you need to fly to Guatemala to collect. Remember, it's your diet. Make it work for you.

3   Keep a food diary. Or keep using that checklist—it sounds boring and a bit obsessive, but it can be a great tool to help you stay on track. It's also symbolic of the fact that you are in charge. Keep an abbreviated version with the first letter of every food category in your diary and check, check, check. Make sure you include exercise in your checklist too. This is a great way to make sure you gain control and not weight! There is a maintenance checklist on page 196.

4   Don't deny yourself. A little of what you fancy does you good; promising yourself you'll never eat another

chocolate cookie is a waste of time—you know it and everyone who knows you knows it too. Healthy weight maintenance is about balance in all things, not denial. It's also about learning to listen to your body. If you're feeling tired or hungry all the time, you may need to reevaluate your calorie needs and move up a notch. If you listen to your body, you'll find you can distinguish between real hunger and emotional need.

5   Don't beat yourself up. If you put a little weight back on one week, it's not the end of the world. Simply refocus and get back to it. Give yourself permission not to be perfect.

6   Stay motivated. Be encouraged by your success and surround yourself with people who want you to succeed. Stay away from diet saboteurs and sustain those positive habits you have adopted. What you eat is important, but it's your positive mind-set that will make it happen. Believe that you can, because you can.

7   Keep your original goals in mind. Why did you want to lose weight in the first place? If you find yourself straying, remember your initial inspiration. Keeping a journal is a great way to reflect on your goals and give yourself a subtle kick along when you need it.

8   Learn to handle stress without turning to food. The things that can lead to weight regain are the stressful events in our lives. When life throws one of those curve balls, staying in control can be a big challenge. Many of us turn to food for comfort, when what we need to do is handle the situation or learn to relax and deal with stress. It's called "comfort food" for a good reason—we feel we are feeding ourselves emotionally when we eat. But often eating makes us feel worse, not better, especially as the pounds pile back on. So in stressful times, stay as calm as you can and in control. You do know the difference between physical hunger and emotional hunger—physical hunger is centered around the stomach while emotional hunger is in the head. If the going gets tough, don't be afraid to seek professional help.

9   Don't skip meals or allow yourself to get too hungry. Eat regular meals—it's an effective tool to keep binge-eating attacks at bay. Eating breakfast seems to be very important. Studies show that people who skip breakfast more than make up for the missed calories throughout the day.

10   Keep moving. Keep up your weight-loss exercise regimen. Lots of research has been done with people who have been successful in maintaining weight loss. The key seems to be exercise. So keep moving and you can keep losing.

What we find incredibly rewarding is to see the transformation in the hundreds of people who have participated in our weight-loss programs since our studies began. They tell us that they can develop a sense of order and control in their lives simply by controlling their food intake and exercising more. Once they start to lose weight and excess fat, their self-esteem soars and they feel energized mentally and physically. Here are some stories to inspire you to keep going.

"I just want to thank the CSIRO for their Total Wellbeing Diet, which I have been following for several months. In that time, I have lost 55 pounds and gone from a size 18 to a size 12. I do not feel at all as if I'm on a diet. I just call it a new eating plan. I love to cook and have been able to experiment with meat and veggies so that every night our dinners are a 'taste sensation.' So thanks for the new approach to eating, which has resulted in a much happier and healthier me."
— *Patricia*

"Over the past seven months I have lost 26–30 pounds. I do combine the eating regime with a daily 3-mile walk. Several friends and relatives are now following the program as a result of my obvious success with it."
— *Brian*

"I have been using your menu plans together with a sensible exercise program for 6 months now and have gone from a size 24 to a size 18 in that time. I consider this type of plan one I can stay with for life."
— *Maria*

## your maintenance plan

Once you've reached your goal, you can begin to add foods so that you no longer lose weight, but maintain it. The keys to success are:

1   maintaining the basic structure of the eating plan, and
2   maintaining your exercise program.

People need different calorie intakes to maintain their weight, even if they are the same age and weight and exercise the same amount. Some people will maintain their weight at a higher calorie level and some will need to be on a lower level. With a little trial and error, you will soon become the best judge as to what works for you.

First of all, this is a good time to recalculate your daily calorie needs—this time for weight maintenance (see Chapter 2). Remember, the basis of all effective weight-loss diets is energy balance and control. When the number of calories you consume in the food and beverages you eat and drink is equal to the number of calories you burn up, your weight will remain stable.

To maintain your weight you can opt to stay on our structured diet program, and simply choose the new Level of the Total Wellbeing diet that is closest to your current calorie maintenance needs. If you like a very structured program, this will probably suit you best until you have the confidence to experiment.

Or you can listen to your body, experiment and slowly add new foods in 120 calorie "blocks" (see table opposite) to your daily menus. We can't emphasize enough how important it is to stick with the basic structure of your eating plan. Our dietitians have found over the years that most people do best with a fairly systematic approach. Here are some guidelines.

• Make sure you include a lean/low-fat protein food serving at each meal.
• Choose whole grain breads and cereals.
• If adding snacks, plan them. Make sure you stay within your block allowance (see below).
• Eat regular meals and always have breakfast (or at least brunch on the weekend!).

Here's how you can add foods in blocks of 120 extra calories a day until you find you are maintaining your weight goal. This approach gives you flexibility—you can choose the same or different foods every day. If you're eating out, you can "save" three of your 120 calorie blocks and enjoy a big night out.

Week 1    Add 120 calories to your basic plan each day.
Week 2    If still losing weight, add another food block of 120 calories to your daily food allowance.
Week 3    Continue to add 120 calorie food blocks each day until you maintain your weight.

What foods to add? We recommend that you buy a good food calorie counter. But to get started, here's a list of foods that our volunteers have found useful.

**EXTRA FOODS TO ADD IN 120 CALORIE BLOCKS**

| food | 120 calorie block |
| --- | --- |
| milk, low-fat | 8 oz |
| bread, whole grain | 1 slice |
| fruit salad, fresh, nontropical | 10 oz |
| almonds, dry-roasted, unsalted | 1 oz |
| potato chips, cooked in sunola oil | 1 oz bag |
| avocado | ¼ whole |
| baked potato | 5 oz |
| pasta, cooked | ⅔ cup |
| lean beef, lamb, chicken or fish | 3.5 oz |
| beans, canned | 4.5 oz |
| cheese | 1 oz |
| cheesecake | 2.5 oz |
| oil | 3 teaspoons |
| ice cream | 2.5 oz |
| chocolate (milk, plain) | 1 oz |
| wine | 5 oz glass |
| beer | 12 oz can |
| spirits | 1.5 oz |

Of course, if you find you are gaining rather than maintaining weight, do not add any foods the following week. If your weight gain is more than 2 pounds, drop back to the previous week's plan. Once you reach the stage where your weight is stable, that should remain your eating plan.

## 5 Weeks on the maintenance plan

Here's a snapshot of how you might incorporate 120 calorie blocks gradually over 5 weeks.

| Week 1 maintenance | Choose any 1 block, e.g., 1 extra-thick slice of toast at breakfast |
|---|---|
| Week 2 maintenance | Choose any 2 blocks, e.g., 1 extra-thick slice of toast at breakfast + nuts as a snack |
| Week 3 maintenance | Choose any 3 blocks, e.g., 1 extra-thick slice of toast at breakfast + nuts as a snack + 1 oz chocolate |
| Week 4 maintenance | Choose any 4 blocks, e.g., 1 extra-thick of slice of toast at breakfast + nuts as a snack + 1 oz chocolate + 1 medium glass of wine |
| Week 5 maintenance | Choose any 5 blocks, e.g., 1 extra-thick slice of toast at breakfast + nuts as a snack + 1 oz chocolate + 1 medium glass of wine + 1 extra serving of fruit |

**Note:** Only continue to add blocks if you are still losing weight. As soon as your weight stabilizes, *stop* adding blocks.

## Keep moving

In the long term, there are many benefits to be gained from regular exercise, both in terms of health and weight management. Exercise forms a perfect partnership with calorie intake, because together they assist in long-term maintenance and prevention of weight regain by increasing calorie output and using excess calories that would otherwise be stored as fat.

# appendices

## appendix 1

**THE TOTAL WELLBEING DIET CHECKLIST**

| week of diet: | Monday | Tuesday | Wednesday | Thursday | Friday | Saturday | Sunday |
|---|---|---|---|---|---|---|---|
| lean dinner protein (7 oz) | | | | | | | |
| red meat 4 times a week | | | | | | | |
| fish twice a week | | | | | | | |
| other once a week | | | | | | | |
| lean lunch protein (3.5 oz) | | | | | | | |
| whole grain bread (2 × 1 oz slices) | | | | | | | |
| fruit (1 medium piece) | | | | | | | |
| fruit (1 medium piece) | | | | | | | |
| high-fiber cereal (1½ oz) | | | | | | | |
| low-fat milk (8 oz) | | | | | | | |
| low-fat yogurt/dessert (8 oz) | | | | | | | |
| salad (½ cup) | | | | | | | |
| vegetable 1 (½ cup) | | | | | | | |
| vegetable 2 (½ cup) | | | | | | | |
| vegetable 3 (½ cup) | | | | | | | |
| vegetable 4 (½ cup) | | | | | | | |
| oil or margarine (3 teaspoons) | | | | | | | |
| low-calorie soup (1 cup) | | | | | | | |
| wine (10 oz) | | | | | | | |
| other | | | | | | | |
| exercise (30 minutes) | | | | | | | |

• note: if on 3 dairy servings (see page 22), use 1½ oz protein plus 1 extra dairy option

# appendix 2

**MAINTENANCE CHECKLIST**

Date:

| week of maintenance plan: | Monday | Tuesday | Wednesday | Thursday | Friday | Saturday | Sunday |
|---|---|---|---|---|---|---|---|
| lean dinner protein (7 oz) | | | | | | | |
| red meat 4 times a week | | | | | | | |
| fish twice a week | | | | | | | |
| other once a week | | | | | | | |
| lean lunch protein (3.5 oz) | | | | | | | |
| whole grain bread (2 x 1 oz slices) | | | | | | | |
| fruit (1 medium piece) | | | | | | | |
| fruit (1 medium piece) | | | | | | | |
| high-fiber cereal (1½ oz) | | | | | | | |
| low-fat milk (8 oz) | | | | | | | |
| low-fat yogurt/dessert (8 oz) | | | | | | | |
| salad (½ cup) | | | | | | | |
| vegetable 1 (½ cup) | | | | | | | |
| vegetable 2 (½ cup) | | | | | | | |
| vegetable 3 (½ cup) | | | | | | | |
| vegetable 4 (½ cup) | | | | | | | |
| oil or margarine (3 teaspoons) | | | | | | | |
| low-calorie soup (1 cup) | | | | | | | |
| wine (10 oz/week) | | | | | | | |
| 120 calorie "block" | | | | | | | |
| 120 calorie "block" | | | | | | | |
| 120 calorie "block" | | | | | | | |
| exercise (30 minutes) | | | | | | | |

• note: if on 3 dairy servings (see page 22), use 1½ oz protein plus 1 extra dairy option

# appendix 3

**U.S. FOOD AND NUTRITION BOARD DIETARY REFERENCE INTAKES (DRIS):**

**RECOMMENDED INTAKES OF VITAMINS AND MINERALS***

| nutrient | individual amount | pregnant/breast-feeding women | women over 50 |
|---|---|---|---|
| vitamin A | 700–900 μg (micrograms) | 770/1300 μg | 700 μg |
| vitamin C | 75–90 mg | 85/120mg | |
| thiamin | 1.1–1.2 mg | 1.4/1.4 mg | |
| riboflavin | 1.1–1.3 mg | 1.4/1.6 mg | |
| niacin | 14–16 mg | 17/18 mg | |
| calcium | 1000–1200 mg | | |
| iron | 8-18 mg | 27/9 mg | |
| vitamin D | 10 μg | 5/5 μg | 15 μg |
| vitamin E | 15 μg | 15/19 μg | |
| vitamin B6 | 1.0–1.5 mg | 1.9/2.0 mg | |
| folic acid | 400 μg | 500/500 μg | |
| vitamin B12 | 2.4 μg | 2.6/2.8 μg | |
| phosphorous | 700 mg | | |
| iodine | 150 mg | 220/290 mg | |
| magnesium | 320–420 mg | 360/320 mg | |
| zinc | 8–11 mg | 11/12 mg | |
| copper | 900 μg | 1000/1300 μg | |
| biotin | 30 mg | 30/35 mg | |
| pantothenic acid | 5 mg | 6/7 mg | |

* From Dietary Reference Intakes (DRIs): Recommended Intakes for Individuals, Vitamins and Minerals, 2002
(source: http://www.nal.usda.gov/fnic/etext/000105.html)

# appendix 4

## results of the CSIRO study diets

Fifty-one women tested the higher protein, low-fat diet and 49 women tested the higher carbohydrate, low-fat diet. Since both diets were low in fat, we'll refer to them as the higher protein and higher carbohydrate diets.

Weight loss

- The higher protein group lost on average 16.8 pounds over 12 weeks; 45 out of 51 women in this group lost more than 8.8 pounds over the 12 weeks.
- The higher carbohydrate group lost on average 15.2 pounds over 12 weeks; 39 out of the 49 women in this group lost more than 8.8 pounds over the 12 weeks.
- Women with high triglyceride levels (more than 136 mg/dl) lost on average more weight (17.6 pounds) on the higher protein diet than on the higher carbohydrate diet (13.2 pounds).
- Actual fat loss for women on the higher protein diet was on average 13.2 pounds; those on the higher carbohydrate diet lost on average 6.6 pounds. The amount of weight lost from the midriff area was twice as high on the higher protein diet (2.2 pounds versus 1.1 pounds).

Compliance

- There were 5 dropouts from the higher protein diet but 16 dropouts from the higher carbohydrate diet during the first 12 weeks. At 3 months, 3 more had dropped out of the higher carbohydrate group, but no more had dropped out of the higher protein group.

Nutrients

- The vitamin B12 status of the women in the higher protein group increased significantly over 12 weeks compared with average levels. The vitamin B12 status of the women in the higher carbohydrate group decreased over the same period.
- Hemoglobin levels improved for the women on the higher protein diet and remained the same for the women on the higher carbohydrate diet.

Bone turnover markers

- Women on both diets had increased bone turnover.
- Women on both diets had decreased calcium excretion.

Cardiovascular disease risk

- Triglyceride levels fell by 13 percent in women on the higher-protein diet but were not significantly different for women on the higher carbohydrate diet.
- Women with initial high triglyceride levels experienced a 28 percent reduction in triglyceride levels on the higher protein diet, compared with 10 percent on the higher carbohydrate diet.
- LDL cholesterol fell on average by 4.8 percent in women on either diet.
- HDL cholesterol fell on average by 7 percent in women on either diet.
- Blood glucose levels fell on average by 4 percent in women on either diet.
- Blood insulin levels fell on average by 20 percent in women on either diet.

Please visit www.csiro.au for more information on the scientific background to the Total Wellbeing Diet. For the full study method and results, see: Noakes, M., Keogh, J.B., Foster, P.R., Clifton, P.M. Effect of an energy-restricted high-protein diet relative to a conventional high-carbohydrate low-fat diet on weight loss, body composition, nutritional status and markers of cardiovascular health in obese women. *American Journal of Clinical Nutrition* 2005. This particular study was funded by Meat & Livestock Australia.

Here is a list of scientific papers on higher protein diets that CSIRO Health Science and Nutrition has published.

Noakes, M., Clifton, P.M. Changes in plasma lipids and other cardiovascular risk factors during three energy-restricted diets differing in total fat and fatty acid composition. *American Journal of Clinical Nutrition* 2000, 71(3): 706–12.

Noakes, M., Clifton, P.M. Weight loss and plasma lipids. *Current Opinion in Lipidology* 2000, 11(1): 65–70.

Luscombe, N.D., Clifton, P.M., Noakes, M., Parker, B., Wittert, G. Effects of energy-restricted diets containing increased protein on weight loss, resting energy expenditure, and the thermic effect of feeding in type 2 diabetes. *Diabetes Care* 2002, 25(4): 652–57.

Parker, B., Noakes, M., Luscombe, N., Clifton, P. Effect of a high-protein, high-monounsaturated fat weight-loss diet on glycemic control and lipid levels in type 2 diabetes. *Diabetes Care* 2002, 25(3): 425–30.

Farnsworth, E., Luscombe, N.D., Noakes, M., Wittert, G., Argyiou, E., Clifton, P.M. Effect of a high-protein, energy-restricted diet on body composition, glycemic control, and lipid concentrations in overweight and obese hyperinsulinemic men and women. *American Journal of Clinical Nutrition 2003,* 78(1): 31–39.

Luscombe, N.D., Clifton, P.M., Noakes, M., Farnsworth, E., Wittert, G. Effect of a high-protein, energy-restricted diet on weight loss and energy expenditure after weight stabilization in hyperinsulinemic subjects. *International Journal of Obesity* 2003, 27(5): 582–90.

Moran, L.J., Noakes, M., Clifton, P.M., Tomlinson, L., Norman, R.J. Dietary composition in restoring reproductive and metabolic physiology in overweight women with polycystic ovary syndrome. *Journal of Clinical Endocrinology and Metabolism* 2003, 88(2): 812–19.

Noakes, M., Clifton, P.M. Weight loss, diet composition and cardiovascular risk. *Current Opinion in Lipidology* 2004, 15: 31–35.

Bowen, J., Noakes, M., Clifton, P.M. A high–dairy protein, high-calcium diet minimizes bone turnover in overweight adults during weight loss. *Journal of Nutrition* 2004, 134: 568–73.

Brinkworth, G.D., Noakes, M., Keogh, J.B., Luscombe, N.D., Wittert, G.A., Clifton, P.M. Long-term effects of a high-protein, low-carbohydrate diet on weight control and cardiovascular risk markers in obese hyperinsulinemic subjects. *International Journal of Obesity* 2004, 28(9): 1187.

Clifton, P.M., Noakes, M., Keogh, J.B. Very low-fat (12%) and high monounsaturated fat (35%) diets do not differentially affect abdominal fat loss in overweight, nondiabetic women. *Journal of Nutrition* 2004, 134(7): 1741–45.

Moran, L.J., Noakes, M., Clifton, P.M., Wittert, G.A., Tomlinson, L., Galletly, C., Luscombe, N.D., Norman, R.J. Ghrelin and measures of satiety are altered in polycystic ovary syndrome but not differentially affected by diet composition. *Journal of Clinical Endocrinology and Metabolism* 2004, 89(7): 3337–44.

Brinkworth, G.D., Noakes, M., Parker, B.A., Clifton, P.M. Long-term effects of substituting protein for carbohydrate in a low-fat diet on weight loss and cardiovascular risk markers in obese subjects with type-2 diabetes. *Diabetologia* 2004, 47(10): 1677–86.

Bowen, J., Noakes, M., Clifton, P.M. Effect of calcium and dairy foods in high-protein, energy-restricted diets on weight loss and metabolic parameters in overweight adults. *International Journal of Obesity* 2005.

Luscombe-Marsh, N.D., Noakes, M, Wittert, G.A., Keogh, J.B., Foster, P., Clifton, P.M. Carbohydrate-restricted diets either high in monounsaturated fat or high in protein are equally effective at promoting fat loss and improving blood lipids. *American Journal of Clinical Nutrition* 2005.

# appendix 5

## Cooking meat and fish

With so much to choose from, how do you select the meat or fish that is right for your dish? And when you get it home, how do you cook it and for how long? Below is a guide to the best cuts of meat and types of fish for particular dishes; and following that are cooking tips that will give you great results.

| Cooking method | suitable beef cuts | suitable veal cuts | suitable lamb cuts | suitable chicken cuts | suitable pork cuts | suitable types of fish |
|---|---|---|---|---|---|---|
| Barbecue/ Pan-fry/Grill | filet, rib eye, sirloin, t-bone, rump, round, blade | chops, cutlets, scaloppine, tenderloin | trim lamb steaks (round or topside) cutlets, eye of loin, filet, loin chops | whole bird butterflied, leg (thigh or drumstick), breast, wings | lean pork (steaks, chops, slices, strips), belly pork, ribs, filet | whole fish, filets or steaks – with skin on. Barbecue or grill firm-fleshed, oilier (usually dark-fleshed) fish, such as mullet or tuna; pan-fry delicate textured and flavored (usually white-fleshed) fish, such as John Dory and cod. |
| Stir-fry | filet, rib eye, rump, sirloin, topside, round | | eye of loin, filet, round or topside | boneless thigh, breast | lean pork (steaks, chops, slices, strips), belly pork, ribs, filet | pieces of firm-fleshed fish filet, such as swordfish |
| Roast | rib eye, scotch filet, rump, sirloin, filet, topside, silverside, blade, round | leg (boned or bone in) topside, silverside or round; loin (boned or bone in); boned shoulder | leg (bone in or easy carve), shoulder (boned and rolled or easy carve), boned and rolled loin, round roast, topside roast, neck filet roast, trim eye of loin, loin rack, party rack, four rib roast | whole bird, leg (thigh or drumstick), breast, wings | leg (bone in or boned), knuckle, rump, loin (bone in or boned), rack, shoulder, filet | whole fish, filets or steaks of all types |
| Casserole | chuck, brisket, topside, round, blade, silverside | leg, shoulder, neck, brisket, shank | diced lamb forequarter, forequarter chops, shanks | leg (thigh or drumstick), breast | neck, leg (topside, rump, silverside), boned shoulder | pieces of firm-fleshed fish filet, such as mako, bluefish and swordfish |

The following cooking tips will help you to produce perfectly cooked meat or fish each time.

Barbecue/pan-fry/grill
- If the recipe allows it, lightly coat the meat or fish with oil instead of adding oil to the pan. This will reduce the amount of oil needed and assist in sealing in the juices.
- Ensure the cooking surface is hot—there should be lots of sizzle when the meat or fish hits the surface.
- Place the meat or fish on the surface (skin-side down first, if applicable) and let it cook until moisture appears on the top surface, then turn it (once only).

Red meat steaks: only buy steaks of even thickness (at least ¾ inch thick); if using a pan, it should be heavy based; do not poke, prod or pierce the meat during cooking as this will dry it out.

*Rare*—cook for a few minutes each side; turn only once; cook until steak feels "very soft" when pressed with the back of tongs.
*Medium*—cook on one side until moisture is pooling on top surface; turn only once; cook on second side until moisture is visible; cook until steak feels "springy" when pressed with back of tongs.
*Well done*—cook on one side until moisture is pooling on top surface; turn and cook on second side until moisture is pooling on top; reduce heat slightly and continue to cook until steak feels "very firm" when pressed with back of tongs.

After cooking, place steaks in a warm place or cover with foil and rest for 3–5 minutes.

Stir-fry
- Ensure the wok or frying pan is hot before you add the oil.
- Wait until the oil is hot before you add the meat or fish— there should be lots of sizzle when the meat hits the oil.
- Stir-fry meat or fish in small batches (about 7 oz at a time) to keep the pan hot and prevent the meat from stewing.
- Remove meat or fish from pan and stir-fry remaining ingredients.
- Return meat or fish and add any sauces.
- Heat through and serve immediately.

Roast
- Preheat the oven.
- If the roast is a filet, brown it in a little oil on the stove top before roasting.
- Place roast in a baking dish (or seal it in a foil parcel).
- Cook roast in the oven: the following times for red meat are a guide only. Baste frequently.
- Remove roast when cooked to your liking and cover with foil.
- Let rest for 10–20 minutes before carving. (Not necessary for fish.)

## SUGGESTED ROASTING TIME PER 1 POUND MEAT

| | temp | rare | medium | well-done |
|---|---|---|---|---|
| **BEEF** | | | | |
| rib eye, scotch filet, rump, sirloin, filet, topside | 395°F | 15–20 mins | 20–25 mins | 25–30 mins |
| london broil, chuck, round | 320°F | 20–25 mins | 25–30 mins | 30–35 mins |
| **LAMB** | | | | |
| leg (bone in or easy carve), shoulder (boned and rolled or easy carve), boned and rolled loin, trim lamb tunnel-boned leg | 350°F | 20–25 mins | 25–30 mins | 30–35 mins |
| round roast, topside roast, neck filet roast, trim lamb eye of loin | 430°F | 30–35 mins | 35–40 mins | 40–45 mins |
| loin rack, party rack, four rib roast | 395°F | 30–35 mins | 35–40 mins | 40–45 mins |

Casserole

- If the recipe allows it, lightly coat meat or fish in oil instead of adding oil to a pan. This will reduce the amount of oil needed and assist in sealing in the juices.
- Brown meat or fish in a deep-sided pan in small batches (about 7 oz at a time) to keep the pan hot and prevent the meat from stewing.
- Sauté spices, then add liquid and slow-cooking vegetables, such as potatoes and carrots.
- Bring to the boil then reduce heat to low and simmer, covered, for approximately 2 hours for red meat (1 hour for chicken and pork and 10–20 minutes for fish).
- Add quick-cooking vegetables, such as peas and mushrooms, in the last 20 minutes of cooking.

Range of information kindly provided by Meat & Livestock Australia

# appendix 6

## Shopping lists

The shopping lists on the following pages cover all the foods used in the menu plans on pages 67–89. Use the lists as they are if you are following the menu plans exactly, or amend them slightly if you have personalized the plans to include your favorite foods.

"In the cupboard" is a list of commonly used ingredients that appear in the menu plans and recipes. You will need these ingredients, daily or weekly, in order to follow the menu plans, but most of them are cooking staples and you will probably find that you already have them in your cupboard or fridge. If not, pick up the rest at your local supermarket before you begin the menu plans.

## In the cupboard . . .

fruit (canned)
dried fruit (apples, raisins)

frozen peas
onions (brown, pearl, red)
potatoes
garlic
ginger

eggs

low-fat milk
low-fat flavored yogurt
dairy desserts (low-fat custard, low-fat
   ice cream, etc.)

whole grain bread
whole grain bread rolls
crispbreads
breakfast cereals (including oatmeal, high-fiber
   cereal)
short-grain rice

anchovy filets

baby capers
balsamic vinegar
white-wine vinegar
flour
cornstarch
brown sugar
white sugar
Equal (or other artificial sweetener)
cocoa
vanilla
stock (beef, chicken, vegetable)
spices (allspice; freshly ground black pepper;
   cardamom—ground, seeds & pods; chili
   powder; garam masala; chinese five-spice
   powder; cinnamon—ground & sticks; cloves;
   coriander—ground & seeds; cumin—ground;
   fennel—ground; lemon pepper; turmeric;
   nutmeg—ground; paprika; saffron)
dried herbs (bay leaves, oregano)
light margarine
low-calorie jam
mustard (whole grain, Dijon)
oil-free mayonnaise
oil-free salad dressing

horseradish
barbecue sauce
ketchup
tomato paste
canned tomatoes
baked beans
tandoori paste
pesto
chutney
pickles
cranberry sauce
olive oil
olive oil spray
peanut oil
sesame oil
soy sauce
oyster sauce
hoisin sauce
dry sherry (Chinese rice wine)
fish sauce
orange juice
red wine
white wine

These "Weekly shopping lists" in combination with the "In your cupboard" list will provide you with all you need to follow the 12-week menu plans of the Total Wellbeing Diet.

The amounts needed of foods will depend on how many people in the household are on the diet and/or how many people are eating the suggested main meals. Copy these pages and fill in the required quantities.

## Week One

fresh fruit (including bananas, lemons, limes, pineapple)
asparagus
avocado
carrots (baby)
broccoli
bok choy
chili peppers (small red)
cucumbers
green beans
herbs (basil, cilantro, flat-leaf parsley, mint, oregano, tarragon, thyme)
lettuce (romaine)
mushrooms (button, field)
peas
peppers (green, red, yellow)
salad leaves (mixed-leaf, arugula)
squash (butternut)
tomatoes (including Roma)
zucchini
canned salmon
salmon filets
swordfish steaks
skinless chicken breasts
lean bacon
sliced lean ham
sliced corned beef
beef filet
lamb filet
rack of lamb
low-fat feta
whole grain raisin bread
kalamata olives

## Week Two

fresh fruit (including bananas, lemons, oranges, strawberries)
beets
broccoli
carrots
celery
chili peppers (red)
cucumbers
herbs (basil, cilantro, mint, flat-leaf parsley, rosemary)
leeks
mushrooms (button, shiitake)
rhubarb
salad leaves (mixed-leaf)
scallions
snow peas
squash (butternut)
tomatoes
zucchini
smoked salmon
snapper filets
tuna steaks
white fish filets
skinless chicken thigh filets
sliced turkey
lean bacon
sliced lean ham
diced beef
sirloin
rack of veal
lamb leg
low-fat cheddar cheese
low-fat cream cheese
low-fat natural yogurt
frozen spinach
pine nuts
powdered skim milk
canned white cannellini beans

## Week Three

fresh fruit (including apples, bananas, lemons, oranges)
asparagus
avocado
beets
broccoli
carrots
cauliflower
celery
herbs (basil, parsley, rosemary, tarragon)
eggplants (baby)
green beans
leeks
lettuce (romaine)
mushrooms (button)
parsnips
peppers (red)
rhubarb
salad leaves (mixed-leaf, arugula)
scallions
tomatoes (including cherry)
zucchini
canned fish (salmon, tuna)
swordfish steaks
skinless chicken breasts
sliced lean ham
sliced roast beef
lean ground beef
veal cutlets
lamb leg
lamb loin chops
low-fat cheddar cheese
full-fat cheddar cheese
parmesan
low-fat yogurt (natural, vanilla)
whole grain raisin bread
kalamata olives
pine nuts

## Week Four

fresh fruit (including lemons, limes, pears)
bean sprouts
beets
broccoli
broccolini
carrots
celery
chili peppers (red, green)
cucumbers
fennel bulbs
green beans
herbs (basil, cilantro, mint, flat-leaf parsley, rosemary, tarragon)
mushrooms (button, field)
peas
peppers (red)
salad leaves (baby spinach, mixed-leaf, arugula)
scallions
squash (butternut)
tomatoes (including Roma)
smoked salmon
flathead filets
snapper filets
calamari
mussels
shrimp
skinless chicken breasts
sliced lean ham
pastrami
sliced roast beef
lean ground beef
rump steak
beef filet
sirloin
lamb cutlets
lamb filets
light cream cheese
low-fat cheddar cheese
full-fat cheddar cheese
low-fat natural yogurt
parmesan
blue cheese
whole grain raisin bread
pine nuts

## Week Five

fresh fruit (including lemons, limes, oranges)
avocado
bok choy
broccoli
carrots
chili peppers (red)
cucumbers
green beans
herbs (basil, cilantro, oregano, flat-leaf parsley)
lettuce (romaine)
mushrooms (field)
peppers (green, red)
rhubarb
salad leaves (mixed-leaf, arugula)
scallions
tomatoes (including Roma)
canned salmon
canned tuna
sardines
white fish filets
skinless chicken breast
sliced turkey
pastrami
sliced roast beef
lean ground beef
diced lean beef
lamb filets
lamb steaks
low-fat cheddar cheese
low-fat feta
low-fat ricotta
whole grain raisin bread
whole grain crumpets
whole grain Lebanese flatbreads
kalamata olives
sesame seeds

## Week Six

fresh fruit (including bananas, lemons, limes, oranges)
avocado
bean sprouts
bok choy
broccoli
carrots
celery
chili peppers (red)
cucumbers
green beans
herbs (basil, cilantro, mint, flat-leaf parsley, rosemary)
mushrooms (button)
peas
peppers (red)
pickles
salad leaves (baby spinach, mixed-leaf, arugula)
scallions
spinach
squash
sweet potatoes
tomatoes
canned salmon
salmon steaks
white fish filets
skinless chicken thigh filets
sliced lean ham
sliced roast beef
rump steaks
lean ground beef
lamb filets
leg of lamb
low-fat cheddar cheese
low-fat feta
low-fat ricotta
low-fat yogurt (natural, vanilla)
rye bread
foccacia bread
whole grain sourdough bread
whole grain bagels
mango chutney
pitted green olives
red miso paste
sesame seeds

## Week Seven

fresh fruit (including lemons, limes)
avocado
beets
bok choy
broccoli
carrots
celery
chili peppers (red)
cucumbers
eggplant
green beans
herbs (basil, cilantro, oregano, flat-leaf parsley, rosemary, sage)
mushrooms (button)
peppers (red, yellow)
salad leaves (baby spinach, mixed-leaf, arugula)
snow peas
squash (butternut)
tomatoes (including cherry, Roma)
zucchini
canned salmon
sardines
flathead filets
calamari
mussels
shrimp
chicken tenderloins
skinless chicken breasts
lean bacon
sliced lean ham
pastrami
lean ground beef
veal steaks
full-fat cheddar cheese
low-fat ricotta
multigrain English muffins
whole grain English muffins
whole grain Lebanese flatbreads
flaked almonds
herb mustard
honey
sesame seeds
tabouli

## Week Eight

fresh fruit (including bananas, lemons, limes, oranges)
asparagus
avocado
broccoli
broccolini
carrots (including baby)
cauliflower
celery
chili peppers (green)
green beans
herbs (basil, cilantro, mint, flat-leaf parsley, rosemary, tarragon, thyme)
leeks
mushrooms (button, shiitake)
peas
peppers (red)
salad leaves (mixed-leaf)
scallions
snow peas
squash (butternut)
tomatoes
canned tuna
canned salmon
salmon filets
white fish filets
skinless chicken thigh filets
sliced lean ham
sliced corned beef
sirloin
lean ground beef
lamb filets
rack of lamb
full-fat cheddar cheese
whole grain raisin bread
whole grain English muffins
whole grain pita bread
pine nuts

## Week Nine

fresh fruit (including lemons, limes)
alfalfa sprouts
avocado
baby bok choy
carrots
chili peppers (red)
cucumbers
eggplants (baby)
herbs (basil, cilantro, mint, flat-leaf parsley, sage)
lettuce (romaine)
mushrooms (button)
peppers (green, yellow)
salad leaves (baby spinach, mixed-leaf, arugula)
scallions
tomatoes (including Roma)
zucchini
canned salmon
smoked salmon
snapper filets
tuna steaks
sardines
sliced turkey
sliced lean ham
pastrami
veal steaks
lamb loin chops
lamb steaks
low-fat cheddar cheese
low-fat feta
low-fat ricotta
parmesan
whole grain raisin bread
whole grain Lebanese flatbreads
whole grain English muffins
cashews
kalamata olives

## Week Ten

fresh fruit (including bananas, lemons,
    oranges)
avocado
bean sprouts
beets
bok choy
broccoli
carrots
chili peppers (red)
cucumbers
eggplant
green beans
herbs (basil, cilantro, lemongrass, mint,
    oregano, flat-leaf parsley, rosemary)
mushrooms (button)
peppers (red, yellow)
pickles
salad leaves (mixed-leaf, arugula)
snow pea sprouts
squash (butternut)
tomatoes (including cherry, Roma)
zucchini
canned salmon
swordfish steaks
skinless chicken breasts
lean bacon
sliced lean ham
sliced roast beef
rump steaks
sirloin
lamb filets
full-fat cheddar cheese
low-fat cheddar cheese
low-fat ricotta
low-fat natural yogurt
rye bread
whole grain sourdough bread
whole grain bagels
whole grain English muffins
kalamata olives
pickled onions
star anise

## Week Eleven

fresh fruit (including lemons, oranges)
avocado
beets
broccoli
carrots
cauliflower
celery
cucumbers
green beans
herbs (basil, flat-leaf parsley, rosemary)
mushrooms (button, shiitake)
peppers (red, yellow)
pickles
salad leaves (baby spinach, mixed-leaf, arugula)
scallions
snow peas
squash
sweet potatoes
tomatoes (including Roma)
zucchini
canned tuna
smoked salmon
swordfish steaks
white fish filets
skinless chicken breasts
sliced turkey
sliced lean ham
pastrami
lean ground beef
sirloin
rack of veal
lamb shanks
full-fat cheddar cheese
low-fat cheddar cheese
mozzarella
parmesan
cinnamon-and-raisin bagels
rye bread
whole grain English muffins
whole grain Lebanese flatbreads
chopped jalapenos
kalamata olives
canned three-bean mix

## Week Twelve

fresh fruit (including lemons)
bean sprouts
broccoli
Brussels sprouts
carrots
cauliflower
celery
cucumbers
fennel bulbs
green beans
herbs (basil, cilantro, mint, oregano, flat-
    leaf parsley, rosemary, tarragon, thyme)
mushrooms (button, field)
peas
peppers (red)
salad leaves (baby spinach, mixed-leaf, arugula)
scallions
snow peas
tomatoes
zucchini
canned tuna
sardines
white fish filets
skinless chicken breasts
sliced lean ham
sliced roast beef
diced lean beef
rump steaks
lamb cutlets
leg of lamb
full-fat feta
low-fat natural yogurt
rye bread
whole grain sourdough bread
whole grain Lebanese flatbreads
frozen spinach
powdered skim milk
canned corn

# index